ELIMINATE

THE

COMPETITION

The Business and Art of Aesthetic Practice

Also By John Zannis, MD

Tales for Tagliacozzi – An Inside Look at Modern-Day Plastic Surgery

Cut to the Chase : Essential Cosmetic Surgery Information for Every Patient

Body Contouring Without Surgery

ELIMINATE

THE

COMPETITION

The Business and Art of Aesthetic Practice

JOHN ZANNIS, MD

Amphora
Publishing

ELIMINATE THE COMPETITION: The Business and Art of Aesthetic Practice

Contact the publisher: info@amphorapublishing.com

Contact the author: www.zannis.com

Book Cover by Amphora Designs

Published by: Amphora Publishing | First edition 2024.

ISBN: 979-8-9908111-0-2

9 798990 811102

Imprint: Amphora Publishing

Dedicated to my children:

Gabriella, Alexander, Christopher

CONTENTS

PREFACE

As a business owner, sometimes competition really sucks. You work your butt off, spend a ton on advertising, dedicate yourself to excellence, and then someone else does the same thing. . . only for a lower price.

So, what do you do? Work harder, run a sale, mark down your prices, and gain some new attention and customers. And then the cycle continues until every similar business in your market has raced to the bottom and your margins are barely capable of sustaining you.

It's a common scenario, and the precise reason why many businesses can't make it. It may be good for the consumer – lots of choices, elevated service, cheaper prices – but how is the business owner going to survive, let alone thrive?

There is a much better way. It's the way all superior companies defy the odds and become the leader in their sector. It's why many try to compete, but there is only one Apple, or one Nike. Their strategy is to become not only the market leader, but the *only viable option* in the minds of millions of consumers. Those companies have no competition.

How did they accomplish this amazing feat? Is it possible to use the same tactics in a small business? Absolutely! Once I discovered this, my business not only grew, it exploded. And, it was more fun and more effortless. Let me explain.

I started my business career as a medical doctor. This is not a very suitable background for running a corporation. I was in my mid-30s, with a wife and two young kids, and we had just moved to a small town in eastern North Carolina with the goal of starting a solo private practice in plastic surgery. It was an exciting prospect, and my entrepreneurial instincts were much more suited to building something than joining an existing company and becoming an employee.

Nevertheless, the fact remained that no one had ever trained me in the world of business. My undergraduate degree was in art and human biology. Medical school prepared me well for surgical residency. And my residency in plastic surgery did an amazing job at providing experience and in-depth hands-on education on being a competent plastic surgeon. But like many others, I had to figure out all the business parts on my own. How do you start a professional corporation? How do you file for an employee identification number? What types of insurance will I need? What are the laws dictating the structure of my company?

After the logistics of setting up the business, there was finding and upfitting a building, interviewing and hiring staff, and credentialing with insurance companies.

At last, I was ready to see patients. Where were they? Oh right, marketing, search engine optimization, networking, word of mouth, open house. . .

I was fortunate to be the only plastic surgeon in my town and there was a pent-up demand for my services. The surgical practice grew rapidly and after 3 years, I expanded by opening a med spa.

The med spa was a great complement to my practice because the aestheticians helped manage the skin care needs, and we offered massages and other treatments for a more wholistic approach to wellness. Meanwhile, it also created a new set of challenges: a much bigger staff (most of them independent contractors), more retail and merchandising needs, and much more local competition. In addition, many "aesthetic practices" were now offering cosmetic procedures at their medical clinics or day-spas.

Fast forward several years, and the med spa had become profitable. I learned spa management well. More importantly, I developed critical business skills essential for success that apply to every sector, particularly those in the service industry. **It was the *Eliminate the Competition* strategy that led to unparalleled growth and profits.**

When you realize that competition is actually amazing, and it only helps keep you at the top when you are the best, you invite it. New competition only highlights why you are the best and reinforces your position as the leader. It would require a lot to remove Rolls Royce from the pedestal it's on.

Learn how to be the best in every area of your business. Offer a unique experience and unmatched customer service. Your reputation will emerge as the only aesthetic practice worth visiting. You will have the opportunity to grow and serve many customers.

Although the concept is simple, the execution is not. In this book, I draw from my own experience, and also highlight many examples of other successful corporations and individuals in the field. I hope this in-depth guide to the aesthetic business will allow you to avoid many of the struggles I experienced early on, and give you a shortcut to the future you dream of.

With hard work and determination, anyone can do it.

You just need to know how!

John Zannis, MD

New Bern, NC

Introduction to the

Eliminate the Competition Approach

Understanding the Need for Business Coaching in the Aesthetic Industry

All great performers or athletes require an equally great coach. Overconfidence in skills we don't truly possess invariably leads to failure. Especially when dealing with accomplished surgeons or business executives, company leaders often eschew coaching or mentorship. One reason may be the perception that it is an unnecessary expense. More commonly it is misunderstanding of what business coaching is or unawareness of its value.

Business coaching, especially if within your niche, is critical to high-level success, and this is often learned too late. I'm not trying to sell you anything right now. That's why I wrote this book: to provide as much high-level value and specific action steps as possible to supercharge your aesthetic practice. But aside from this book, there are amazing supplemental courses and mentorships for those looking to dominate. I too resisted coaching until I saw how powerful it was for a different physician in my industry (more details on this later).

In today's competitive world, the aesthetic industry is booming, with new clinics and practices opening up every day. Plastic surgeons, aesthetic medicine doctors, dermatologists, cosmetologists, aestheticians, and many other professionals are competing for a piece of the 20-billion-dollar aesthetic industry. And, the forecasted market size is staggering!

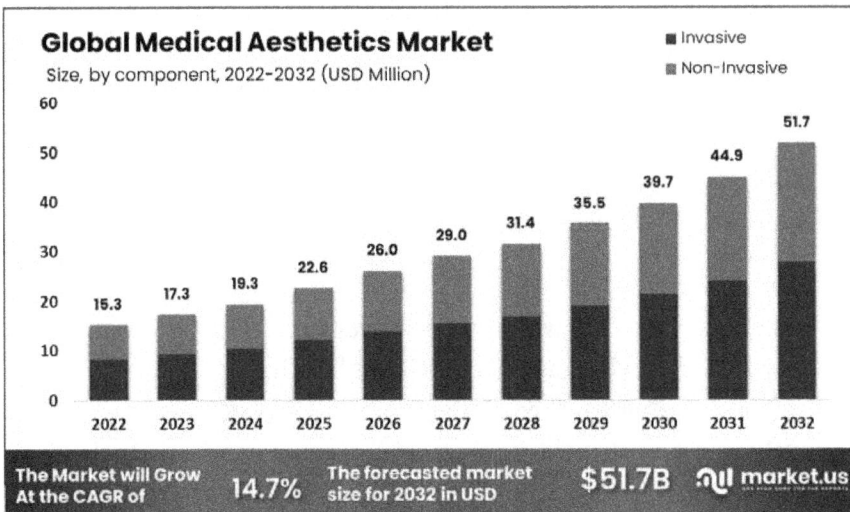

Global Medical Aesthetics Market
Size, by component, 2022-2032 (USD Million)

- Invasive
- Non-Invasive

Year	Value
2022	15.3
2023	17.3
2024	19.3
2025	22.6
2026	26.0
2027	29.0
2028	31.4
2029	35.5
2030	39.7
2031	44.9
2032	51.7

The Market will Grow At the CAGR of **14.7%** The forecasted market size for 2032 in USD **$51.7B** market.us

Figure 1. Forecasted Medical Aesthetics Market Size. Source: https://www.globenewswire.com/news-release/2023/09/15/2743909

As an owner, it is crucial to stay ahead of the game and ensure the success of your company. This is where business coaching for aesthetic practitioners comes into play.

When I started out on my own journey 15 years ago, I had very little help and no experience with running a business. I learned what I could from online sources and books, but it was trial and error and persistence that taught me how to succeed in the aesthetic business. In residency, I learned how to be a plastic surgeon. In solo private practice, I learned how to be a great plastic surgeon and businessman who could run an efficient operation and scale for higher earning potential. But ultimately, I plateaued. I couldn't see a way to scale greater, and I didn't have any interest in bringing on partners.

That's when coaching changed everything for me. I discovered Bedros Keuilian through his YouTube channel (www.youtube.com/@BedrosKeuilian), and began following the business advice he shared through his video content and podcast. He talked about scaling any business to over $200 million dollars! There was no way *my* particular business, a medical practice and med-spa, could scale to that height. Was franchising the way to go? Did I need more providers? Well, long story short, I learned how Bedros helped one of his coaching clients, an aesthetic and wellness doctor, triple her revenue in just one year. I dug in deeper and began coaching sessions of my own.

Franchising definitely was not the answer for me. It was rethinking the way I could affect change in patients' lives beyond surgery. This included online teaching, virtual consultations, publications, and becoming a thought leader in my field. Intellectual property can exist and sell *ad infinitum.* The margin on such products is absurd and part of the way I superscaled my business activity.

Since that epiphany, I have successfully founded 5 different businesses and taken them to over $17 million dollars in value.

My Path to Becoming a Business Coach

Over the past several years, the roles have reversed, and I teach what I have learned. I have become a high-level marketing advisor and aesthetic business coach for those looking to bypass the struggle and fast-track their own path to success. Even with time and toil, you are not guaranteed success. Some people never learn what it takes or develop the acumen to thrive in today's marketplace. As a serial entrepreneur, I know exactly what it takes to make it big. **There is a very clear path to creating a multimillion-dollar enterprise, and I have distilled this path into a blueprint for anyone to utilize.**

It still takes talent, smarts, and effort, but most important is the core knowledge that you can implement into your business strategy. Without knowing what to do, you are destined to fail. I want you to succeed. But not just succeed; I want you to *dominate* your market by totally *eliminating all competition*! That's how you **guarantee** winning. And no, I'm not worried about giving out this information or it affecting my profits because I have no competition!

Michael Jordan could create a detailed masterclass of his workout regimen and techniques that would help student develop their game and take it to new heights. But, there will always be only one Michael Jordan.

One of the key advantages of business coaching is the ability to gain a fresh perspective on your practice. Often, as medical professionals, we become so engrossed in the day-to-day operations that we lose sight of the bigger picture. A coach can help you step back, assess your goals, and develop a strategic plan to achieve them. By providing an outsider's viewpoint, they can identify areas of improvement and offer innovative solutions to enhance your practice's efficiency and profitability.

Running a successful aesthetic practice obviously requires more than just medical or cosmetic expertise. It requires a comprehensive understanding of marketing, branding, customer service, financial management, and strategic planning. These are the areas where business coaching can make a significant difference and help you achieve all your professional aspirations. It also helps with the intangible aspects that are best learned one on one: charisma, attitude, positivity, body language, accountability, social aptitude, etc.

Attract & Retain Clients

One of the primary reasons why business coaching is essential for aesthetic practitioners is the need to attract and retain clients. I prefer to use the phrase *create clients* because it is a proactive process that puts you in control of your destiny. You can't succeed without happy, returning clients, and what better way to ensure that happens than creating them? In a saturated market, it can be challenging to stand out from the competition. As a coach, I would help you create a strong personal brand identity, develop effective marketing strategies that are proven and cost-effective, and enhance your online presence to build a massive following of loyal fans. By understanding your target audience and their needs, you can deliver exactly what they need to achieve the results they desire. Choosing the smallest viable market and then over-serving them will always lead to winning.

Financial Management

Managing finances is another critical aspect of running any successful company. Many medical professionals lack the necessary financial knowledge to effectively manage their business. An experienced coach who's managed finances can provide guidance on creating a comprehensive financial plan, tracking key performance indicators, and managing cash flow. By implementing sound financial practices, you can optimize your revenue, reduce expenses, and ultimately increase profitability. Using modern strategies to earn money while you sleep, you'll have more free time to focus on your family and other interests, and your revenue potential will be limitless. This was one of my greatest revelations!

Strategic Planning

In addition to marketing and financial management, you will need clear strategic planning. You need to be realistic, but your goals don't have to be. Goals should be huge, or they will never materialize. A good coaching system creates an actionable plan, and holds you accountable for achieving those goals. By developing a clear vision for your practice and implementing strategic initiatives, you can accomplish anything.

Leadership Skills

Business coaching can also improve your leadership skills. As a cosmetic surgeon or medical spa owner, you are responsible for leading your team and creating a positive work environment. Improving your communication skills helps with creating clients, team building, and conflict resolution, ultimately resulting in a more motivated and productive team. Having a successful role model to imitate is a great start.

Networking and Connections

Finally, an often-overlooked advantage of having an established coach is networking and connections. Business coaches often have extensive networks and connections within their industries. They can introduce you to potential partners, investors, mentors, or other professionals who can help you grow quickly or more efficiently. These connections can open doors to new opportunities and expand your professional circles.

I believe business coaching for aesthetic practitioners is crucial in today's competitive market. By understanding the need for comprehensive business knowledge and guidance, cosmetic surgeons and medical spa owners can enhance their marketing efforts, improve financial management, develop strategic plans, and become effective leaders. Investing in coaching and learning the tools required for success will be the absolute **best investment you ever make**!

Overview of the Eliminate the Competition Approach

With my plug for coaching officially over, let's dive into the strategy you can initiate right now on your own. In the highly competitive world of cosmetic surgery and medical spas, it is essential for aesthetic business owners to have a clear strategy for success. The most effective approach to help you stay ahead of the curve is what I call the *Eliminate the Competition* approach. Here is an overview of this powerful strategy and how it can benefit cosmetic surgeons and medical spa owners in particular.

The Eliminate the Competition approach is rooted in the belief that to achieve long-term success, it is crucial to differentiate yourself from your competitors. With the rise in demand for aesthetic procedures, the market has become increasingly saturated with providers offering similar services. To stand out and attract clients, you must develop a unique selling proposition (USP) that sets you apart.

Here are my 7 steps to guide you through the process of identifying your USP, hiring the right people, branding yourself, and leveraging these steps to eliminate the competition: *FINESSE.*

1. Find Your People: This first step underscores the importance of placing the right people in the right roles before determining the strategic direction of your company. This means hiring individuals who are not only skilled but also aligned with the company's core values and culture. There is no compromise on personnel decisions, and the right people must be in roles where their strengths are maximized.

2. Innovation: Staying ahead of the curve is essential in the aesthetic industry. Later, I will discuss the importance of constantly innovating your services and incorporating the latest advancements in technology to offer a superior experience to your clients. Additionally, customers searching for trending procedures and the latest products will find your practice if it is publicizing those items.

3. Niche: By focusing on a specific niche or procedure, you can position yourself as an expert in that area. This allows you to target a specific audience and become the go-to provider for that particular treatment. You don't necessarily want to pigeonhole yourself, but patients always prefer a specialist over a generalist. Why go to the surgeon that does some rhinoplasties when you can see the one that does *only* rhinoplasties? A med spa with an entire laser department and laser-only operators sounds much more likely to deliver a good result than one that has a laser in a room that occasionally gets used.

4. Exceptional Customer Service: Providing exceptional customer service could be the single most significant differentiating factor. We will delve into techniques for creating a personalized and memorable experience for your clients, ensuring they become loyal advocates for your practice. There's nothing more unique in a selling proposition than demonstrating how you are the only one who provides a certain level of care and why you are the only one who can provide a certain experience because of the very nature of who you are (experience, special training or rare talents) or your environment (unique location, historic building, one-of-a-kind facility).

5. Self-Promotion and Strategic Partnerships: Effective self-promotion is crucial for both personal and business growth. Some of the best techniques we consider include: creation of your website to stand out, most effective utilization of social media platforms, developing and sharing valuable content online, networking, personal branding, and consistent messaging.

Collaborating with other businesses, such as skincare product manufacturers or wellness centers, can help expand your reach and enhance your reputation. We will explore how to identify and establish mutually beneficial partnerships to eliminate competition and increase your market share. This also includes online collaborations with influencers and organizations that have their own abundant source of followers whose demographic or interests overlap with yours.

6. Scaling: In essence, scaling is about growing the business sustainably and efficiently, ensuring that it can handle increased demand and opportunities without faltering. It may involve entering new markets or expanding product lines to attract a broader customer base. Another aspect may be automation or streamlining operations to improve efficiency.

7. Evolving and Adapting: Fostering a culture of experimentation, leveraging customer feedback, adopting agile development practices, making data-driven decisions, and maintaining lean practices during scaling are key strategies that will help you to navigate uncertainty, adapt to changing market conditions, and achieve sustainable success in an ever-evolving world.

By implementing the Eliminate the Competition approach, you will *FINESSE* yourself into a position of leadership in the industry, attract more clients, and ultimately increase your profitability. This book will provide you with the necessary tools, strategies, and case studies to inspire and guide you on your journey towards total domination of your market!

FINESSE

Finding Your People and Your Way

Chapter 1

Find Your People

"You don't build a business, you build people, then people build the business."

— Zig Ziglar

The success of any business hinges on various factors, including market conditions, competitive strategies, and innovative capabilities. However, one critical element often overlooked is the importance of having the right people in the right roles *before* determining the strategic direction. This principle, emphasized in Jim Collins' seminal work *Good to Great*,[1] underpins the foundation of sustainable success for any organization. So, let's begin by exploring the many ways in which ensuring the right people are in the right roles can significantly influence a company's strategic direction and overall success.

The Concept of "First Who, Then What"

In *Good to Great*, Jim Collins introduces the concept of "First Who, Then What," which asserts that getting the right people on board is a prerequisite for figuring out the strategic direction of a company. According to Collins, great companies first focus on who they bring onto their team before deciding what direction to take. This approach contrasts with the traditional view where strategy formulation often precedes talent acquisition and deployment.

---

[1] Collins, Jim. *Good to Great: Why Some Companies Make the Leap... and Others Don't*. Harper Business, 2001.

The Foundation of Success: People Over Strategy

Building a Robust Organizational Culture

A company's culture is a reflection of its people. When the right individuals, who share common values and a commitment to excellence, are in place, a strong, positive culture naturally develops. This culture becomes the bedrock upon which the company's strategies are built. A cohesive culture fosters collaboration, innovation, and resilience, enabling the company to adapt to changes and overcome challenges more effectively.

Figure 2. Finding and hiring the right people is one of the most important first steps for a business.

Enhancing Team Dynamics and Performance

The right people in the right roles enhance team dynamics and performance. Teams with the right mix of skills, experiences, and personalities are more likely to work well together, communicate effectively, and achieve their goals. Such teams can leverage their collective strengths, compensate for individual weaknesses, and maintain high levels of motivation and engagement. This alignment and synergy are critical for executing strategic initiatives successfully.

Ensuring Accountability and Responsibility

Having the right people in the right roles ensures that each team member is accountable and responsible for their specific tasks. When roles are clearly defined and matched with individuals' strengths and competencies, it leads to greater ownership and accountability. This clarity in roles and responsibilities minimizes overlaps and gaps, streamlines decision-making processes, and enhances overall organizational efficiency.

Aligning Talent with Strategic Objectives

Identifying Core Competencies

Before determining strategic direction, it is crucial to understand the core competencies of the organization. This understanding begins with recognizing the strengths and capabilities of the people within the organization. By placing individuals in roles that align with their core competencies, companies can better leverage their human resources to achieve strategic objectives. This alignment ensures that the strategic direction is realistic, achievable, and sustainable.

Facilitating Strategic Agility

Organizations with the right people in the right roles are more agile and adaptable. When a company is composed of talented, versatile individuals, it can pivot more quickly in response to market changes, technological advancements, or competitive pressures. This strategic agility is essential for maintaining a competitive edge in a rapidly changing business environment.

Driving Innovation and Creativity

Innovation is often a product of diverse perspectives and collaborative problem-solving. By placing the right people in roles where they can thrive, companies foster an environment conducive to creativity and innovation. Employees who feel valued and appropriately challenged are more likely to contribute innovative ideas and solutions that can drive the company forward.

Case Studies: Success Through People

Apple Inc.: The Right People for Revolutionary Innovation

Apple Inc. is a prime example of the importance of placing the right people in the right roles. Under Steve Jobs' leadership, Apple consistently attracted and retained top talent who were passionate about innovation and excellence. Jobs' focus on hiring individuals who not only had the technical skills but also aligned with Apple's vision and culture was instrumental in the company's success. The result was groundbreaking products like the iPhone, iPad, and MacBook, which revolutionized the tech industry and cemented Apple's position as a market leader.

Southwest Airlines: A People-Centric Approach

Southwest Airlines is another example of a company that prioritizes people over strategy. The airline's founder, Herb Kelleher, believed that happy and engaged employees would lead to satisfied customers and a successful business. By focusing on hiring individuals who fit the company's culture of fun, dedication, and customer service, Southwest was able to create a unique and resilient business model. This people-centric approach has helped the airline maintain profitability and customer loyalty in a highly competitive industry.

Challenges in Implementing "First Who, Then What"

Identifying the Right People

One of the primary challenges in implementing the "First Who, Then What" approach is identifying the right people. This involves not only assessing candidates' skills and experiences but also their cultural fit and alignment with the company's values. It requires a thorough and often time-consuming recruitment and selection process.

Role Clarity and Job Design

Ensuring that individuals are in the right roles also requires clear job descriptions and effective job design. Companies must invest in understanding the specific requirements of each role and how they align with the overall organizational goals. This may involve restructuring roles and responsibilities to better match the strengths and capabilities of existing employees.

Managing Resistance to Change

Implementing this approach may encounter resistance from within the organization, especially if it involves significant changes in roles and responsibilities. Employees may be hesitant to move out of their comfort zones or may fear job insecurity. Effective change management strategies, including clear communication, training, and support, are essential to overcome this resistance.

Strategies for Successful Implementation

Comprehensive Recruitment and Selection Process

A comprehensive recruitment and selection process is crucial for identifying the right people. This process should go beyond assessing technical skills and experience to evaluate cultural fit, values alignment, and potential for growth. Techniques such as behavioral interviews, psychometric testing, and situational judgment tests can provide deeper insights into candidates' suitability for specific roles.

Continuous Development and Training

Investing in continuous development and training ensures that employees remain competent and capable of meeting evolving business needs. Providing opportunities for skill development, career advancement, and leadership training helps in retaining top talent and preparing them for future challenges.

Effective Performance Management

An effective performance management system aligns individual performance with organizational goals. Regular feedback, performance reviews, and development plans help in identifying areas for improvement and recognizing high performers. This system should also be flexible enough to accommodate changes in roles and responsibilities as needed.

Fostering a Positive Organizational Culture

A positive organizational culture that values collaboration, innovation, and continuous improvement is essential for the "First Who, Then What" approach. Leaders play a crucial role in shaping and sustaining this culture by modeling desired behaviors, recognizing and rewarding contributions, and fostering an inclusive and supportive work environment.

The Role of Leadership in "First Who, Then What"

Visionary Leadership

Visionary leaders understand the importance of placing the right people in the right roles before determining the strategic direction. They have a clear vision of where they want to take the organization but recognize that achieving this vision requires a talented and committed team. These leaders focus on building a strong team first and trust that the right strategy will emerge from the collective wisdom and capabilities of their people. More on this in the next chapter.

Servant Leadership

Servant leaders prioritize the growth and well-being of their team members. They focus on empowering and enabling their employees to perform at their best. By placing the right people in the right roles, servant leaders ensure that their team members have the support and resources they need to succeed, which in turn drives the organization's success.

Transformational Leadership

Transformational leaders inspire and motivate their teams to achieve extraordinary outcomes. They recognize the potential in their employees and strive to align individual aspirations with organizational goals. By ensuring that people are in roles where they can thrive and contribute meaningfully, transformational leaders create a high-performing and engaged workforce capable of driving the organization's strategic direction.

Summary

The principle of "First Who, Then What" underscores the critical importance of placing the right people in the right roles before determining the strategic direction of a business. This approach builds a strong foundation for sustainable success by fostering a positive organizational culture, enhancing team dynamics and performance, ensuring accountability, and aligning talent with strategic objectives.

Companies like Apple Inc. and Southwest Airlines demonstrate how prioritizing people over strategy can lead to exceptional performance and competitive advantage. However, implementing this approach requires careful consideration, including identifying the right people, ensuring role clarity, managing resistance to change, and fostering a supportive organizational culture.

Leadership plays a pivotal role in this process, with visionary, servant, and transformational leaders driving the successful implementation of the "First Who, Then What" principle. By focusing on their people first, these leaders create the conditions for strategic clarity, agility, innovation, and long-term success.

In a rapidly changing and competitive business landscape, the importance of having the right people in the right roles cannot be overstated. It is the foundation upon which great companies are built and the key to achieving and sustaining greatness.

Chapter 2

Vision & Goals: Foundations for Success

"The only thing worse than being blind is having sight but no vision."

— Helen Keller

Introduction to Vision and Goals

In the world of aesthetic practice ownership, success often hinges on the ability to navigate a complex landscape with clarity and purpose. I know you are ready to jump into the fun stuff: designing your building, trending procedures and services, marketing and brand, social media, and the money! Those will come soon, I promise. And though it is a little tedious, clarifying the purpose for your business will set you on course for success. Success is a journey, and at the heart of this journey lies the interplay between vision and goals—a dynamic duo that propels everyone towards their aspirations. But what exactly do I mean by vision and goals, and how do they shape the trajectory of an aesthetic practice?

Although it may be helpful, I hate it when instructional or self-help books say: "Take out a paper and a pen and write down your vision for. . ." or "your top 3 business goals. . ." Yes, writing these down could make them more real and more lasting in your subconscious mind, but at least for now, just *think* about them.

Vision represents the guiding light that illuminates the path ahead—a beacon of clarity amidst uncertainty. It encapsulates the essence of **why we do what we do**, providing a compelling narrative that inspires action and fuels ambition. A well-defined vision serves as the North Star,

28

guiding practitioners through the ebbs and flows of entrepreneurship, anchoring them to their core values and aspirations.

Goals, on the other hand, are the **steppingstones that transform vision into reality**. They are the tangible manifestations of our aspirations, breaking down the grand vision into actionable steps and measurable outcomes. Whether short-term or long-term, goals provide a roadmap for progress, driving focus, accountability, and momentum.

The Significance of Vision

In the bustling landscape of aesthetics, clarity is king. A crystal-clear vision not only illuminates the path forward but also serves as a magnetic force, attracting like-minded individuals and opportunities that resonate with our purpose. Clients are drawn to businesses that understand their purpose and that pursue it with passion. A clear vision also keeps you away from money-losing ventures that don't support your overarching purpose.

Case Study: Dr. Smith's Vision for Patient-Centric Care

Consider the story of Dr. Emily Smith, a visionary cosmetic surgeon whose practice thrives on a foundation of patient-centric care. Dr. Smith's vision is simple yet profound: to empower individuals to embrace their unique beauty and reclaim their confidence. This vision permeates every aspect of her practice, from the warm smiles that greet patients at the reception desk to the innovative treatments tailored to their specific needs.

Dr. Smith's commitment to her vision extends beyond the walls of her practice, shaping her engagement with the community and industry at large. Through educational workshops, philanthropic initiatives, and thought leadership contributions, she champions a holistic approach to beauty that transcends superficial ideals. Dr. Smith's unwavering dedication to her vision not only sets her apart in a crowded market but also earns her the trust and loyalty of her patients—a testament to the transformative power of clarity and purpose.

Goals as Roadmaps to Success

While vision provides the destination, goals chart the course—a roadmap to success in an ever-changing landscape. Whether aiming to expand services, increase revenue, or enhance patient satisfaction, goals serve as actionable milestones that propel practitioners towards their vision.

Setting SMART Goals:

The SMART criteria—Specific, Measurable, Achievable, Relevant, Time-bound—serve as a guiding framework for goal-setting, ensuring that objectives are clear, attainable, and aligned with the overarching vision. Let's break down each component:

• **Specific**: Clearly define the objective, avoiding vague or ambiguous language.

Example: Increase the number of manicures performed each month by promoting our unique services.

• **Measurable**: Establish quantifiable metrics to track progress and success.

Example: Increase the number of manicures performed each month by 15 by promoting our unique services on Facebook, X, Instagram, and TikTok.

• **Achievable**: Set goals that are realistic and within reach, considering available resources and constraints. Modify your goal if necessary.

Example: Increase the number of manicures performed each month by 15 by promoting our unique services on Facebook, X, and Instagram.

• **Relevant**: Ensure that goals align with the broader vision and strategic priorities of the practice. Why are you setting the goal that you're setting?

Example: Increase the number of manicures performed each month by 15 by promoting our unique services on Facebook, X, and Instagram.

Because manicures and pedicures are the most common spa service sought after in our community, there are more potential customers and the possibility to dramatically increase traffic through the spa.

• **Time-bound**: Assign deadlines or timelines to create a sense of urgency and accountability. When will the team start creating and implementing the tasks they've identified? When will they finish?

Example: Increase the number of manicures performed each month by 15 by then end of the fiscal year by promoting our unique services on Facebook, X, and Instagram. Because manicures and pedicures are the most common spa service sought after in our community, there are more potential customers and the possibility to dramatically increase traffic through the spa.

By applying the SMART criteria to goal setting, you can transform abstract aspirations into concrete actions, and maximize impact.

The Interplay Between Vision, Mission, and Goals

While vision, mission, and goals are distinct concepts, they are intrinsically interconnected, forming a symbiotic relationship that drives progress and growth. Understanding the interplay between these elements is key to shaping your business trajectory.

HOW TO IDENTIFY YOUR GOALS

VISION   GOALS   MISSION

Figure 3. How Goals Relate to Vision & Mission

Iterative Refinement: The Evolution of Vision and Goals

In the dynamic landscape of aesthetic practice ownership, change is the only constant. As practitioners navigate shifting market trends, technological advancements, and evolving patient preferences, their vision and goals must adapt accordingly. This iterative process of refinement involves continuous reflection, adjustment, and realignment to ensure alignment with the ever-changing landscape of public demand.

Consider the journey of Dr. James Lee, a seasoned medical spa owner whose vision of delivering cutting-edge skincare solutions has evolved over the years. What began as a modest aspiration to provide quality treatments has blossomed into a bold vision of pioneering innovation in the field of non-invasive aesthetics. Dr. Lee's goals have likewise evolved in tandem with his expanding vision, encompassing objectives such as research and development, staff training, and strategic partnerships to propel his practice to new heights.

Visionary Leadership: Inspiring Alignment and Action

At the helm of every successful aesthetic practice is a visionary leader who embodies the essence of the practice's vision and galvanizes others to share in its pursuit. Visionary leadership goes beyond mere words—it is a way of being that permeates every interaction, decision, and initiative, inspiring alignment and action at every level of the organization.

Take the example of Dr. Sarah Patel, whose unwavering commitment to her vision of inclusivity and diversity has transformed her cosmetic surgery practice into a beacon of empowerment and acceptance. Through her authentic leadership style, Dr. Patel fosters a culture of openness, respect, and collaboration, where every team member feels valued and empowered to contribute their unique talents towards a shared purpose.

Crafting Your Vision

With a deeper understanding of the foundational role of vision and goals in shaping the trajectory of an aesthetic practice, let us now turn our attention to the process of crafting a compelling vision—one that reflects our purpose, values, and aspirations, while resonating with our target audience and market niche.

Start by reflecting on your personal values and the purpose behind starting or running your business. Consider what drives you, what you believe in, and what impact you want your business to make in the world. Since a written mission statement is important, jot down some ideas for each of these categories; it will make crafting the mission statement much easier.

1. Articulating Purpose

At the heart of every successful practice lies a sense of purpose—an intrinsic motivation that fuels our passion and propels us forward in our journey. Articulating this purpose is the first step towards crafting a compelling vision that inspires action and resonates with our audience.

Consider the story of Dr. Sophia Nguyen, a visionary cosmetic surgeon whose journey began with a simple yet profound desire to help others feel comfortable in their own skin. Dr. Nguyen's purpose-driven approach to practice ownership is evident in every aspect of her work, from the personalized care she provides to her patients to the community outreach programs she spearheads to promote body positivity and self-acceptance.

By reflecting on the deeper meaning behind their work, practitioners like Dr. Nguyen can articulate a clear and compelling purpose that serves as the foundation of their vision—a beacon of inspiration that guides their actions and defines their impact on the world.

2. Identifying Target Audience and Market Niche

Understanding the needs, preferences, and aspirations of our target audience is essential to crafting a vision that resonates with their hearts and minds. By identifying our ideal patients and market niche, we can tailor our vision to address their unique challenges and aspirations, creating a powerful connection that fosters loyalty and engagement. This is also a critical first step in product / service development and marketing.

3. Understanding Your Ideal Patients

To identify your target audience, start by painting a vivid picture of your ideal patients or clients. Consider factors such as age, gender, socioeconomic status, lifestyle, and aesthetic goals. What motivates them to seek aesthetic treatments? What are their pain points, aspirations, and values? By delving deep into the psyche of your ideal

patients, you can gain invaluable insights into how to position your practice and tailor your messaging to resonate with them on a personal level.

Take, for example, Luxe Aesthetics, a high-end medical spa catering to affluent clientele in urban centers. Dr. Alexandra Reynolds, the founder of Luxe Aesthetics, recognized early on the importance of understanding her target audience—the affluent, discerning individuals who prioritize luxury, convenience, and exceptional results.

By leveraging market research and demographic analysis, Dr. Reynolds identified the specific needs and preferences of her ideal patients, from their desire for discreet, concierge-style service to their penchant for cutting-edge treatments with minimal downtime. Armed with this deep understanding, she crafted a vision for Luxe Aesthetics that positioned the practice as the premier destination for luxury aesthetic experiences, where every detail is meticulously curated to delight and pamper discerning clientele.

4. Defining Your Market Niche

In addition to understanding your target audience, it's essential to identify your market niche—the specialized segment of the market where your practice can differentiate itself and excel. Whether it's a focus on a particular treatment modality, aesthetic specialty, or patient demographic, carving out a distinct niche allows you to establish expertise, build credibility, and attract a loyal following.

Case Study: Specializing in Non-Surgical Body Contouring at Sculpted Beauty

Consider Sculpted Beauty, a boutique medical spa specializing in non-surgical body contouring treatments. Dr. Michael Chen, the founder of Sculpted Beauty, recognized the growing demand for non-invasive alternatives to traditional liposuction and saw an opportunity to carve out a niche in this rapidly expanding market segment.

By focusing exclusively on non-surgical body contouring, Dr. Chen positioned Sculpted Beauty as a leader in the field, offering a range of innovative treatments tailored to the unique needs of his patients. From state-of-the-art radiofrequency devices to cutting-edge cryolipolysis technology, Sculpted Beauty became synonymous with safe, effective, and transformative body sculpting solutions, attracting clients from across the region seeking to enhance their physique without surgery.

5. Tailoring Your Vision to Your Audience and Niche

Once you've gained a deep understanding of your target audience and market niche, it's time to tailor your vision to align with their needs, preferences, and aspirations. Your vision should speak directly to the desires and pain points of your ideal patients, positioning your practice as the solution they've been searching for.

6. Uncovering Unique Value Proposition

In a crowded marketplace, differentiation is key to standing out and capturing the attention of potential patients. Your unique value proposition (UVP) is what sets your practice apart from competitors and compels patients to choose you over alternatives. By uncovering and articulating your UVP, you can carve out a distinct identity in the market and attract patients who resonate with your offering.

7. Defining Your Unique Value Proposition

Your UVP encompasses the unique benefits and advantages that your practice offers to patients. It goes beyond the services you provide and encompasses the entire patient experience, from the moment they first encounter your brand to their ongoing relationship with your practice. To define your UVP, consider the following questions:

• What makes your practice different from others in the market?

• What specific benefits do you offer that address the needs and desires of your target audience?

• How do you deliver value to patients in a way that competitors cannot replicate?

Case Study: Radiant Smiles Dental Spa

Radiant Smiles Dental Spa, led by Dr. Maya Patel, has differentiated itself in the competitive dental industry by offering a unique blend of dental care and spa-like amenities. Dr. Patel's practice goes beyond traditional dental services, providing patients with a relaxing and rejuvenating experience from the moment they walk through the door.

From aromatherapy and massage chairs in the waiting room to complimentary facials and hand treatments during appointments, Radiant Smiles Dental Spa has redefined the patient experience. Dr. Patel's UVP centers around personalized care and attention to detail, creating a sanctuary where patients can receive top-quality dental treatment while indulging in moments of self-care and relaxation.

8. Communicating Your Unique Value Proposition

Once you've defined your UVP, it's essential to communicate it effectively to your target audience. Your UVP should be front and center in your branding, messaging, and marketing efforts, ensuring that patients understand what sets you apart and why they should choose your practice.

Case Study: Branding and Messaging at Glow Medical Aesthetics

Glow Medical Aesthetics, founded by Dr. Jessica Wong, has built its brand around the concept of natural beauty enhancement. Dr. Wong's practice offers a range of non-invasive cosmetic treatments designed to enhance patients' natural features and boost their confidence.

Through strategic branding and messaging, Glow Medical Aesthetics communicates its UVP of natural beauty enhancement to prospective patients. From its logo and website design to its social media content and advertising campaigns, every touchpoint reinforces the practice's commitment to helping patients look and feel their best while maintaining a natural appearance.

9. Evolving Your Unique Value Proposition

As market dynamics shift and patient preferences evolve, it's essential to continuously evaluate and evolve your UVP to remain relevant and competitive. Regularly solicit feedback from patients, monitor industry trends, and stay attuned to changes in the competitive landscape to ensure that your UVP remains compelling and differentiated.

10. Defining Core Values and Ethical Principles

At the heart of every successful aesthetic practice lies a set of core values and ethical principles that guide decision-making, shape culture, and define the practice's identity. By defining and upholding these values, practitioners can build trust with patients, foster a positive work environment, and differentiate their practice in the marketplace.

11. Identifying Core Values

Core values represent the fundamental beliefs and principles that govern how a practice operates and interacts with patients, staff, and the community. They serve as the moral compass that guides decision-making and shapes behavior at every level of the organization. To identify your practice's core values, reflect on the following questions:

- What principles are most important to you and your team?

- What qualities do you want your practice to be known for?

- How do you want patients to perceive your practice?

Case Study: Integrity and Excellence at Elite Plastic Surgery

Elite Plastic Surgery, led by Dr. Thomas Johnson, is renowned for its commitment to integrity and excellence in patient care. Dr. Johnson's practice operates with transparency, honesty, and integrity, ensuring that patients are fully informed and empowered to make educated decisions about their treatment options.

From the initial consultation to post-operative care, every interaction at Elite Plastic Surgery is guided by the highest standards of professionalism and ethics. Dr. Johnson's dedication to excellence extends to his team, who undergo rigorous training and adhere to strict protocols to deliver exceptional outcomes and patient satisfaction.

12. Upholding Ethical Principles

In addition to core values, ethical principles form the foundation of ethical practice in aesthetics. Practitioners have a responsibility to uphold ethical standards and prioritize patient safety, informed consent, and confidentiality in all aspects of their practice. By adhering to ethical principles, practitioners build trust and credibility with patients and demonstrate their commitment to professional integrity.

Case Study: Compassion and Empathy at Serenity Medical Spa

Serenity Medical Spa, founded by Dr. Maria Garcia, embodies a culture of compassion and empathy in patient care. Dr. Garcia and her team understand that aesthetic treatments can be deeply personal and sometimes emotionally charged experiences for patients. As such, they approach every interaction with sensitivity, compassion, and respect for the patient's individual needs and concerns.

From providing a supportive environment for patients undergoing transformative procedures to offering compassionate support during recovery, Serenity Medical Spa prioritizes the emotional well-being of patients alongside their physical results. Dr. Garcia's unwavering commitment to ethical principles has earned her practice a reputation for integrity and trustworthiness in the community.

13. Integrating Core Values and Ethical Principles into Practice Culture

Once core values and ethical principles are defined, it's essential to integrate them into the practice's culture and operations. From recruitment and training to performance evaluation and decision-making, core values and ethical principles should serve as guiding principles that inform every aspect of practice management.

Crafting the Vision Statement

With a deep understanding of purpose, target audience, unique value proposition, core values, and ethical principles, it's time to distill these elements into a concise and compelling vision statement. Your vision statement serves as the north star that guides your practice's journey, inspiring stakeholders and aligning efforts towards a common purpose.

Components of a Vision Statement

A well-crafted vision statement typically consists of several key components, but you should focus on these 5 main elements:

1. **Purpose**: Clearly articulate the overarching purpose or mission of your practice.

2. **Target Audience**: Identify the demographic or market niche you aim to serve.

3. **Unique Value Proposition**: Highlight the unique benefits and advantages that set your practice apart.

4. **Core Values**: Articulate the core values that underpin your practice's culture and identity.

5. **Ethical Principles**: Emphasize your commitment to ethical standards and patient-centered care.

Crafting Your Vision Statement

To craft a compelling vision statement, distill the essence of your practice's purpose, values, and aspirations into a concise and impactful message. Your vision statement should be inspiring, memorable, and reflective of your practice's identity and ambitions.

Example Vision Statement: *Beauty Innovations Medical Spa*

"At Beauty Innovations Medical Spa, our vision is to redefine beauty through innovation, compassion, and excellence. We are dedicated to empowering individuals to look and feel their best, embracing their unique beauty with confidence and authenticity. Through cutting-edge treatments, personalized care, and unwavering integrity, we strive to be the premier destination for aesthetic transformation, where every patient feels valued, respected, and empowered to shine."

Communicating Your Vision Statement

Once your vision statement is crafted, it's crucial to communicate it effectively to internal and external stakeholders. Your vision statement should be prominently featured on your website, marketing materials, and internal communications to ensure that everyone within the practice understands and aligns with the overarching vision.

I have nice acrylic signs with our vision statement and core values on the walls of my businesses (primarily in employee areas).

Evolving Your Vision Statement

As your practice grows and evolves, your vision statement may need to be revisited and refined to reflect new goals, priorities, and market dynamics. Regularly revisit your vision statement with key stakeholders, soliciting feedback and insights to ensure that it remains relevant, inspiring, and aligned with the practice's aspirations.

Setting Strategic Goals

Having crafted a compelling vision that encapsulates the purpose, values, and aspirations of your aesthetic practice, the next step is to translate that vision into **actionable** goals. Strategic goals serve as the roadmap that guides your practice's journey towards realizing its vision, providing clarity, focus, and direction along the way. These are specific objectives that can be measured.

Establishing Short-Term Objectives

Short-term objectives are the building blocks of progress, providing immediate direction and momentum towards your long-term vision. By setting SMART (Specific, Measurable, Achievable, Relevant, Time-bound) goals for the near future, you can create a clear pathway for progress and celebrate incremental successes along the way.

Setting SMART Goals

To ensure that your short-term objectives are effective and actionable, it's essential to adhere to the SMART criteria:

• **Specific**: Clearly define the objective, avoiding ambiguity or vagueness.

• **Measurable**: Establish quantifiable metrics to track progress and success.

• **Achievable**: Set goals that are realistic and attainable given available resources and constraints.

• **Relevant**: Ensure that goals are aligned with the broader vision and strategic priorities of the practice.

• **Time-bound**: Assign deadlines or timelines to create a sense of urgency and accountability.

Example Short-Term Goals:

1. Increase patient inquiries by 20% within the next three months through targeted marketing campaigns and referral incentives.

2. Improve patient satisfaction scores by implementing a feedback collection system and addressing areas for improvement within the next six months.

3. Enhance staff training and development programs to improve service quality and efficiency by conducting monthly workshops and seminars.

Case Study: Achieving Short-Term Success at Radiant Skin Clinic

Radiant Skin Clinic, led by Dr. Emily Chen, identified improving patient satisfaction as a short-term goal to enhance the overall patient experience. Dr. Chen and her team implemented a feedback collection system, encouraging patients to provide input on their experiences during and after treatments.

The proactive approach to addressing patient concerns not only improved the patient experience but also strengthened patient loyalty and retention.

Celebrating Short-Term Wins

As you achieve your short-term goals, it's essential to celebrate wins and acknowledge the progress made towards your long-term vision. Whether it's recognizing individual contributions, hosting team celebrations, or sharing success stories with patients, celebrating milestones fosters a culture of positivity, motivation, and momentum within the practice.

Case Study: Recognizing Achievements at Blissful Beauty Spa

Blissful Beauty Spa, owned by esthetician Sarah Johnson, celebrates short-term wins through monthly team meetings where achievements are recognized and celebrated. Whether it's surpassing revenue targets, achieving high patient satisfaction scores, or implementing successful process improvements, every milestone is acknowledged and celebrated collectively.

By creating a culture of recognition and appreciation, Blissful Beauty Spa fosters a sense of pride and ownership among team members, motivating them to continue striving for excellence and contributing to the practice's success.

Pursuing Long-Term Strategic Goals

While short-term objectives provide immediate direction and momentum, long-term strategic goals set the course for sustained growth and success over time. These goals are the milestones that mark significant achievements and propel your practice towards its overarching vision.

Identifying Long-Term Strategic Goals

Long-term strategic goals should align with your practice's vision and encompass broader objectives that extend beyond immediate operational needs. These goals often encompass areas such as growth, innovation, market expansion, and brand development, positioning your practice for long-term success and sustainability.

Example Long-Term Strategic Goals:

1. Expand practice offerings to include new services or treatment modalities within the next two years to meet evolving patient needs and market demands.

2. Establish strategic partnerships with other healthcare providers or industry stakeholders to enhance referral networks and broaden patient reach within the next five years.

3. Invest in advanced technology and equipment upgrades to maintain a competitive edge and deliver superior patient outcomes over the next decade.

> **Case Study:** Adapting to Market Trends at Radiant Wellness Center
>
> Radiant Wellness Center, owned by Dr. Sarah Patel, recognized the growing demand for holistic wellness solutions, Dr. Patel expanded her practice's offerings to include integrative services such as nutrition counseling, stress management, and mindfulness workshops.

Monitoring Progress and Adjusting Course

As you pursue long-term strategic goals, it's essential to monitor progress regularly and adjust course as needed to stay on track. Market dynamics, competitive landscape, and internal capabilities may evolve over time, necessitating adjustments to your strategic approach to ensure continued alignment with your practice's vision and objectives.

Bonus Goal-setting Techniques

Here are a few other frameworks that you might find useful.

HARD Goals

HARD stands for heartfelt, animated, required, and difficult. This approach harnesses the emotional aspect of achieving a goal to drive motivation. It prompts individuals to link their goals to a sense of necessity and pushes them to establish challenging and deeply satisfying objectives.

WOOP Goals

WOOP stands for wish, obstacle, outcome, and plan. This method can be particularly effective in breaking habits one wishes to change. It prompts individuals to identify obstacles and devise strategies to overcome them. For example, it can be applied to combat procrastination.

Micro-Goal Technique

Instead of pursuing a single large goal, this approach involves setting numerous small goals that collectively lead to the overarching objective. Attaining these smaller milestones fosters a sense of accomplishment and sustains motivation. Moreover, they serve as regular checkpoints to gauge progress.

Backward Goals

This strategy entails using the desired outcome to determine the steps needed to achieve it. Working backward makes daunting goals more manageable, especially for individuals who have a general idea of what they want but lack clarity. This method breaks down future aspirations into measurable targets.

Locke and Latham's Principles

This technique comprises five key elements aimed at setting effective goals and making progress toward them. These principles include clarity, challenge, commitment, feedback, and task complexity. It is considered one of the most valuable frameworks for goal-setting as it emphasizes the importance of motivation and feedback in tracking progress.

Chapter 3

Leadership: Cultivating a Culture of Excellence

"Leadership is the art of giving people a platform for spreading ideas that work."

— *Seth Godin*

Begin with Strong Leadership

In the aesthetic industry and many other service industries, cultivating a culture of excellence begins with strong leadership. As a cosmetic surgeon or medical spa owner, you set the tone for your practice and establish the standards of professionalism, quality, and service excellence. By fostering a culture where continuous improvement is not only encouraged but expected, you empower your team to strive for excellence in everything they do.

Effective leadership starts with leading by example. As a practice owner, your actions speak louder than words, and your behavior sets the standard for your team. Demonstrating professionalism, integrity, and dedication to patient care sends a powerful message to your staff, inspiring them to emulate your commitment to excellence.

At the end of this chapter, I will offer you a summary of an invaluable insight into the leadership that all companies who go from good to great share: *Level 5 Leadershp*.[2]

---

[2] Collins, Jim. *Good to Great: Why Some Companies Make the Leap... and Others Don't*. Harper Business, 2001.

Dr. Olivia Ramirez, founder of Radiant Skin Clinic, leads by example by consistently delivering exceptional patient care and maintaining high standards of professionalism. Her dedication to continuous learning and professional development inspires her team to stay updated on the latest advancements in aesthetic treatments and customer service best practices.

Empower Your Team

Effective leaders empower their team members to reach their full potential by providing opportunities for growth and development. Invest in ongoing training, mentorship programs, and professional development opportunities to help your staff enhance their skills, expand their knowledge, and advance their careers within your practice.

Sarah Johnson, owner of Blissful Beauty Spa, fosters a culture of learning and growth by offering regular training workshops and encouraging her staff to pursue certifications and advanced training in specialized areas of aesthetics. By investing in her team's development, Sarah not only enhances their skills but also strengthens their commitment to the practice's success.

Communicating with Clarity and Transparency

Clear and transparent communication is essential for effective leadership in the aesthetic industry. As a practice owner, you must ensure that your team understands their roles, responsibilities, and the practice's vision and goals. Establishing open lines of communication fosters trust, collaboration, and alignment, driving the collective efforts of your team towards shared objectives.

Regular Team Meetings: Fostering Collaboration and Alignment

Schedule regular team meetings to provide updates, share important information, and discuss strategic priorities. These meetings offer an opportunity for open dialogue, allowing team members to ask questions, share insights, and contribute to decision-making processes. By fostering a collaborative environment where everyone's voice is heard, you cultivate a sense of ownership and commitment to the practice's success.

Frequent, unnecessary meetings are a waste of time and energy, and not what I'm talking about there. A concise, purposeful meeting with your staff on a regular basis is a motivating tool as well as a housekeeping tool.

At Rinnova Spa & Wellness Center, my spa manager leads a 5 minute huddle every morning to discuss events of the day, highlight an overriding goal (such as promoting a specific service or product), and encourage everyone to have a great day with positive motivation. 5 minutes is all it takes. No grievances, lengthy questions or chit-chat at this morning roundup.

One-on-One Conversations: Providing Individualized Support and Feedback

In addition to group meetings, prioritize one-on-one conversations with your team members to provide personalized support, guidance, and feedback. These interactions offer an opportunity to address individual concerns, celebrate achievements, and identify areas for improvement. By investing time in building strong, one-on-one relationships with your staff, you demonstrate your care for them as an integral part of your business, as well as your commitment to their growth and success within the practice.

Dr. Sophia Nguyen, owner of Renewal Aesthetics Clinic, schedules regular one-on-one meetings with each member of her team to discuss their professional development goals, provide constructive feedback, and offer mentorship. These conversations create a supportive environment where team members feel valued and empowered to excel in their roles. They feel heard and respected and are eager to improve their performance and help the greater cause.

Inspiring Motivation and Engagement

Effective leaders in any industry understand the importance of inspiring motivation and fostering employee engagement. By creating a work environment where team members feel valued, empowered, and motivated to contribute their best efforts, practice owners can drive performance, enhance job satisfaction, and ultimately, deliver exceptional patient care. This is easiest when you have the right people on board (more on acquiring those people later).

Recognition and Appreciation: Celebrating Achievements

Recognizing and appreciating the contributions of your team members is essential for fostering motivation and engagement. Take the time to acknowledge individual and team achievements, whether it's reaching performance milestones, delivering outstanding patient experiences, or going above and beyond in their roles. By celebrating successes and showing gratitude for their efforts, you reinforce a culture of appreciation and positivity within your practice.

Dr. James Lee, owner of Radiant Wellness Center, regularly recognizes his team members for their contributions through employee appreciation events, shout-outs during team meetings, and personalized thank-you notes. By publicly acknowledging their hard work and dedication, Dr. Lee fosters a sense of pride and camaraderie among his staff.

Empowerment and Autonomy: Trusting Your Team

Empowering your team members with autonomy and decision-making authority instills a sense of ownership and accountability in their roles. Trust your staff to make informed decisions and take initiative in their areas of expertise. Encourage them to voice their ideas, experiment with new approaches, and **take ownership** of projects and initiatives. By empowering your team to take ownership of their work, you foster a culture of innovation, creativity, and pride within your practice.

A good example of this process is from the hospitality industry: The Ritz Carleton Hotel. At the Ritz, each employee (or *team member*) from housekeeping to front desk or management, has a significant level of autonomy. They each have a certain dollar amount per quarter at their disposal to be used at their discretion for improving a guest's experience. They also can make on-the-fly decisions that elevate the guest experience without needing to "check with the manager." This is just one example of how you can trust your staff to use good judgement, and in return be rewarded with happier, loyal staff and customers.

Leading Through Change and Uncertainty

In the dynamic and constantly evolving field of aesthetics, effective leaders must navigate change and uncertainty with resilience, adaptability, and strategic vision. Whether it's implementing new technologies, adapting to shifting patient preferences, or responding to industry trends, practice owners must lead their teams with confidence and agility in the face of change. This starts with being well-informed and flexible. It also requires, once again, surrounding yourself with the right people.

Transparency and Open Communication

During times of change and uncertainty, transparency and open communication are essential for maintaining trust and confidence within your team. Keep your staff informed about changes in practice policies, procedures, or strategic initiatives, and provide regular updates on the reasons behind these changes and their potential impact. Encourage open dialogue and feedback to address any concerns or questions your team members may have, fostering a sense of trust and collaboration during periods of transition.

Dr. Jessica Wong, owner of Glow Medical Aesthetics, maintains transparency and open communication with her team during periods of change by holding regular town hall meetings and providing updates via email and internal newsletters. By keeping her staff informed and engaged in the decision-making process, Dr. Wong fosters a culture of trust and transparency within her practice.

Flexibility and Adaptability: Embracing Change as an Opportunity

As a leader, it's essential to demonstrate flexibility and adaptability in response to change. Embrace change as an opportunity for growth and innovation, rather than a threat to the status quo. Encourage your team to embrace change with a positive attitude and a willingness to adapt to new circumstances. Provide support, resources, and training to help your staff navigate change effectively and leverage new opportunities for professional development and practice growth.

Dr. Thomas Johnson, owner of Elite Plastic Surgery, demonstrates flexibility and adaptability by encouraging his team to embrace new technologies and treatment modalities. By investing in staff training and development programs, Dr. Johnson ensures that his team is equipped with the skills and knowledge to adapt to evolving patient needs and industry trends, positioning his practice for long-term success.

Building Trust and Credibility

In the aesthetic industry, more so than many other service industries, trust and credibility are foundational to success. Patients rely on practitioners to provide **safe, effective, and ethical care**, and trust is also essential within the practice among team members. Strong leadership plays a crucial role in building and maintaining trust and credibility, both with patients and within the team.

Integrity and Leading with Honesty

As a practice owner, you must lead with honesty and integrity in all your interactions, whether it's communicating with patients about treatment options and outcomes or addressing concerns and challenges within the team. By demonstrating integrity and transparency in their actions and decisions, leaders foster trust and credibility, earning the respect and confidence of both patients and staff.

Your word may be your most valuable asset. Treat it as such and don't risk tarnishing your reputation by dubious practices or not following through with your commitments. Even through failure, others will support you if you act with integrity and always try to maintain the purity of your word.

Dr. Olivia Ramirez, owner of Radiant Skin Clinic, leads with integrity and transparency by providing patients with honest assessments and recommendations, even if it means recommending less invasive treatments or referring them to other specialists when necessary. By prioritizing patient safety and well-being over profit, Dr. Ramirez earns the trust and loyalty of her patients.

I can attest to this in my own practice. I have always gained more confidence from patients, and consequently more business, when I recommend the best treatment option, even if it is less profitable to the practice. I also frequently suggest they seek a second opinion to feel confident in their decision or secure in my suggested treatment plan. Patients who do this almost always come back to me with gratitude and appreciation for my honesty.

Accountability and Responsibility

Accountability is essential for building trust and credibility within the practice. Leaders must hold themselves and their team members accountable for their actions, decisions, and outcomes. Set clear expectations, establish performance metrics, and provide feedback and support to help your team members meet their responsibilities. By demonstrating accountability in your own actions and holding others to the same standard, you create a culture of responsibility and reliability within your practice.

Dr. Michael Nguyen, owner of Aesthetic Solutions Clinic, emphasizes accountability and responsibility by setting clear performance goals and expectations for his staff. He conducts regular performance reviews and provides constructive feedback to help team members identify areas for improvement and take ownership of their professional development. By fostering a culture of accountability, Dr. Nguyen ensures that his practice delivers consistent, high-quality care to patients.

Leading with Empathy and Compassion

Empathy and compassion are essential qualities of effective leadership, particularly in the aesthetic industry where patient satisfaction and emotional well-being are paramount. Practice owners must lead with empathy and compassion, both towards their patients and their team members, to create a supportive and nurturing environment where everyone feels valued and respected.

Patient-Centered Care: Putting Patients First

Effective leaders in the aesthetic industry prioritize patient-centered care, ensuring that patients feel heard, understood, and cared for throughout their treatment journey. Practice owners must lead by example, demonstrating empathy and compassion in their interactions with patients and empowering their team members to do the same. By putting patients first and prioritizing their needs and preferences, leaders build trust and loyalty, fostering long-lasting patient relationships and positive word-of-mouth referrals.

Dr. Sophia Nguyen, owner of Renewal Aesthetics Clinic, leads with empathy and compassion by taking the time to listen to her patients' concerns, answer their questions, and address their fears and anxieties. She creates a welcoming and supportive environment where patients feel comfortable expressing their emotions and discussing their aesthetic goals, knowing that they are valued and respected.

Supporting Team Well-Being

In addition to prioritizing patient well-being, effective leaders in the aesthetic industry also prioritize the well-being of their team members. Practice owners must lead with empathy and compassion, providing support, encouragement, and resources to help their staff thrive both personally and professionally. By nurturing a supportive environment where team members feel valued, respected, and cared for, leaders foster loyalty, engagement, and job satisfaction, leading to improved staff retention and practice success.

> Dr. Sarah Patel, owner of Radiant Wellness Center, demonstrates empathy and compassion by offering wellness programs, mental health resources, and flexible work arrangements to support her team members' well-being. She encourages open communication and creates opportunities for team bonding and self-care activities to help staff manage stress and maintain work-life balance. By prioritizing staff well-being, Dr. Patel fosters a positive and supportive work environment where team members feel empowered and appreciated.

Embracing Diversity and Inclusion

In the diverse and multicultural landscape of today's world, effective leaders understand the importance of embracing diversity and fostering an inclusive work environment. By embracing diversity in all its forms—whether it's ethnicity, gender, age, or background—you can harness the unique perspectives and talents of your team members to drive innovation, creativity, and success.

Effective leaders prioritize diversity in hiring, ensuring that their team reflects the diverse perspectives and experiences of their patient population. Implement inclusive hiring practices that actively seek out candidates from diverse backgrounds and create opportunities for underrepresented groups to thrive within your practice. By building a diverse team, leaders foster a culture of inclusion and innovation, enhancing the quality of care and service delivery for all patients.

Dr. Jessica Wong, owner of Glow Medical Aesthetics, embraces diversity in hiring by implementing blind recruitment practices and partnering with diversity-focused organizations to attract candidates from underrepresented groups. By actively seeking out diverse talent, Dr. Wong cultivates a culture of inclusion and creativity within her practice, driving innovation and success.

Inclusive Leadership: Empowering All Team Members

Inclusive leaders empower all team members to contribute their unique perspectives and ideas, regardless of their background or identity. Create an inclusive work environment where everyone feels valued, respected, and empowered to speak up and share their thoughts. Foster open dialogue, encourage collaboration, and create opportunities for all team members to participate in decision-making processes. By embracing inclusive leadership practices, leaders foster a culture of belonging and innovation, driving the success of their practice.

Dr. Thomas Johnson, owner of Elite Plastic Surgery, practices inclusive leadership by creating a supportive and inclusive work environment where all team members feel empowered to contribute their ideas and perspectives. He encourages open communication and feedback, and actively seeks out input from team members at all levels of the organization. By valuing diversity and inclusion, Dr. Johnson cultivates a culture of belonging and creativity within his practice.

Navigating Challenges and Adversity

In the competitive and rapidly evolving landscape of the aesthetic industry, effective leaders must navigate challenges and adversity with resilience, adaptability, and strategic vision. Whether it's economic downturns, regulatory changes, or unexpected crises, practice owners must lead their teams with confidence and agility in the face of uncertainty.

Resilient leaders demonstrate optimism and confidence in the face of adversity, inspiring their team members to persevere and overcome challenges. Lead by example, demonstrating resilience in your own actions and decisions, and encourage your team to maintain a positive outlook and focus on solutions rather than dwelling on setbacks. By instilling a sense of resilience and optimism within your team, you foster a culture of perseverance and innovation, enabling your practice to thrive in the face of adversity.

Strategic Vision and Adaptability

Effective leaders in the aesthetic industry anticipate and respond to change with strategic vision and adaptability. Stay informed about industry trends, market dynamics, and emerging technologies, and proactively adapt your practice's strategies and operations to stay ahead of the curve. Encourage innovation and experimentation, and create a culture that embraces change as an opportunity for growth and evolution. By leading with strategic vision and adaptability, practice owners position their teams for success in a rapidly evolving landscape.

Dr. Michael Nguyen, owner of Aesthetic Solutions Clinic, demonstrates strategic vision and adaptability by continuously monitoring industry trends and proactively adapting his practice's services and offerings to meet evolving patient needs. He invests in cutting-edge technologies and treatments, and encourages his team to explore new approaches and techniques to enhance patient outcomes. By leading with strategic vision and adaptability, Dr. Nguyen ensures that his practice remains at the forefront of innovation in the aesthetic industry.

Level 5 Leadership

As promised, I want to share with you an important insight into leadership once again from Jim Collins' *Good to Great.* In the book, which is the culmination of a large study of why some companies make the leap from being good to great and others don't, Collins introduces the concept of Level 5 Leadership. Level 5 leaders possess a unique blend of personal humility and professional will, enabling them to lead their organizations to exceptional long-term success. Here are the key characteristics and components of Level 5 Leadership:

Personal Humility

1. **Modesty**:

   - Level 5 leaders are often understated and modest. They do not seek the spotlight or crave public recognition. Instead, they attribute success to their teams and external factors rather than themselves.

2. **Self-Reflection**:

   - These leaders engage in self-reflection and admit mistakes. They take responsibility for failures, learning from them to avoid repeating errors.

3. **Developing Successors**:

   - They are deeply committed to ensuring the continued success of their companies even after they leave. They mentor and groom successors who can uphold the company's values and vision.

Professional Will

1. **Determination**:

   - Level 5 leaders exhibit an unyielding resolve to do whatever it takes to make the company great. They set high standards and are uncompromising in their pursuit of long-term goals.

2. **Long-term Focus**:

- They focus on building enduring greatness rather than chasing short-term gains. Their decisions are driven by what is best for the company in the long run.

3. **Ambition for the Company**:

- Their ambition is directed towards the institution, not themselves. They prioritize the company's success and legacy over personal fame or fortune.

Duality of Leadership

Level 5 Leadership is characterized by a duality—an almost paradoxical combination of personal humility and professional will. This balance is what sets Level 5 leaders apart from other types of leaders, who might possess strong will but lack humility, or vice versa.

Examples from the Book

Collins provides examples of leaders who embody Level 5 Leadership:

- **Darwin E. Smith** of Kimberly-Clark transformed the company into a leading consumer paper products company despite initially being an unassuming and unexpected choice for CEO.

- **Colman Mockler** of Gillette successfully defended the company from takeover attempts, ensuring its independence and long-term prosperity, driven by a deep commitment to the company's legacy.

The Flywheel Effect

Level 5 leaders understand and harness the "flywheel effect," where consistent, incremental progress accumulates to create a powerful momentum. They focus on building a strong foundation and steadily push the flywheel until the company gains unstoppable momentum.

Summary

Effective leadership is the cornerstone of success in the dynamic and ever-evolving field of aesthetics. As cosmetic surgeons, medical spa owners, and practice leaders, the ability to inspire, motivate, and empower your team is essential for driving innovation, delivering exceptional patient care, and achieving sustainable growth.

Throughout this chapter, we've explored a range of strategies for developing strong leadership skills in the aesthetic industry. From cultivating a culture of excellence and fostering open communication to embracing diversity and leading with empathy, effective leaders in aesthetics understand the importance of nurturing a supportive and inclusive work environment where everyone feels valued, respected, and empowered to contribute their best.

By leading with integrity, transparency, and accountability, practice owners can build trust and credibility with both patients and team members, laying the foundation for long-lasting relationships and practice success. Additionally, navigating challenges and adversity with resilience, adaptability, and strategic vision enables leaders to overcome obstacles and seize opportunities for growth and innovation.

As you continue your journey as a leader in the aesthetic industry, remember that leadership is not a destination but a journey of continuous learning, growth, and improvement. By investing in your own development and the development of your team, you can cultivate a culture of excellence, innovation, and compassion that sets your practice apart and propels it towards greater heights of success.

Level 5 Leadership is a crucial element in the transition from good to great. By combining personal humility with professional will, these leaders create a culture of discipline, commitment, and sustainable success. They lead with quiet strength and determination, prioritizing the organization's long-term health and ensuring its greatness endures beyond their tenure.

Innovation and Technology

Chapter 4

Business Innovation

"The secret of change is to focus all your energy not on fighting the old but on building the new."

— *Socrates*

The Blue Ocean Strategy

Introduction

In the fast-paced and ever-evolving business landscape of the 21st century, innovation is not just a buzzword but a necessity for survival and growth. Businesses constantly face the challenge of staying relevant and competitive amidst rapid technological advancements and shifting consumer preferences. Business innovation involves creating new products, services, or processes that deliver significant value to customers and can disrupt existing markets or create entirely new ones.

Among the myriad strategies for fostering innovation, the "Blue Ocean Strategy" by W. Chan Kim and Renée Mauborgne[3] stands out for its distinct approach to market creation and competition. Unlike traditional strategies that focus on competing within established markets (Red Oceans), Blue Ocean Strategy emphasizes creating new market spaces (Blue Oceans) where competition is irrelevant. This chapter delves into the core principles of Blue Ocean Strategy and explores how businesses can harness its concepts to drive innovation and achieve sustainable growth. The concept fits perfectly with two of

---

[3] Kim, W. C., & Mauborgne, R. (2005). Blue ocean strategy: How to create uncontested market space and make the competition irrelevant. Harvard Business School Press.

the key principles in this book: creating clients and eliminating competition.

Understanding Blue Ocean Strategy

Blue Ocean Strategy is a strategic framework developed by W. Chan Kim and Renée Mauborgne, which was first introduced in their seminal book "Blue Ocean Strategy: How to Create Uncontested Market Space and Make the Competition Irrelevant." The strategy is built on the premise that the market universe consists of two kinds of spaces: Red Oceans and Blue Oceans.

Red Ocean vs. Blue Ocean

- **Red Oceans** represent all the industries in existence today. In these markets, companies try to outperform their rivals to grab a larger share of existing demand. The competition is fierce, and the market space is crowded, leading to a bloody "red ocean" of rivalry.

- **Blue Oceans**, on the other hand, denote untapped market spaces where demand is created rather than fought over. In these markets, competition is irrelevant because the rules of the game are yet to be set. Blue Ocean Strategy advocates for creating these new market spaces to achieve differentiation and low cost simultaneously.

Key Principles of Blue Ocean Strategy

1. **Reconstruction of Market Boundaries**: Blue Ocean Strategy involves looking across traditional industry boundaries to create new market space. This requires companies to challenge conventional assumptions about where industry boundaries lie.

2. **Focus on the Big Picture, Not the Numbers**: Instead of getting bogged down by the competition, companies should focus on the big picture of creating value innovation, which is the simultaneous pursuit of differentiation and low cost.

3. **Reach Beyond Existing Demand**: Companies should aim to unlock new demand by reaching beyond existing customers and tapping into non-customers.

4. **Get the Strategic Sequence Right**: The strategic sequence involves ensuring that the new market offering is compelling and cost-effective, and then building the business model around it.

5. **Overcome Organizational Hurdles**: Implementing a Blue Ocean Strategy requires overcoming key organizational hurdles, such as cognitive, resource, motivational, and political challenges.

6. **Build Execution into Strategy**: Successful implementation of Blue Ocean Strategy necessitates aligning the entire organization with the new strategic vision and ensuring that everyone is committed to executing it.

Creating Uncontested Market Space

The cornerstone of Blue Ocean Strategy is **value innovation**, which aims to create a leap in value for both the company and its customers. This is achieved by simultaneously pursuing differentiation and low cost, breaking the traditional trade-off between the two.

Case Study: Nintendo Wii: Nintendo applied Blue Ocean Strategy with the launch of the Wii. Instead of competing directly with Sony and Microsoft in the high-tech gaming console market, Nintendo created a new market by focusing on casual gamers and families. The Wii offered a unique gaming experience with motion-sensing technology that was easy to use and fun for all ages, creating a new market space.

Value Innovation

- **Differentiation and Low Cost**: Unlike traditional strategies that force a choice between differentiation and cost leadership, value innovation seeks to pursue both simultaneously. This is done by eliminating and reducing factors that the industry takes for granted while raising and creating factors that have never been offered before.

Strategic Tools and Frameworks

To effectively implement Blue Ocean Strategy, Kim and Mauborgne introduced several strategic tools and frameworks that help businesses systematically explore and create Blue Oceans.

Strategy Canvas

The Strategy Canvas is a diagnostic and action framework for building a compelling Blue Ocean Strategy. It captures the current state of play in the known market space and helps companies see where they should focus their efforts.

- **Current Market Space**: The horizontal axis of the Strategy Canvas represents the range of factors that the industry competes on and invests in.

- **Value Curves**: The vertical axis captures the offering level that buyers receive across all these key competing factors.

Case Study: Cirque du Soleil. One of the most famous examples of Blue Ocean Strategy is Cirque du Soleil. Instead of competing with traditional circuses by offering similar acts, Cirque du Soleil created a new form of entertainment that combined elements of theater, opera, and ballet with the circus. This new offering appealed to a whole new set of customers and allowed Cirque du Soleil to charge a premium price, thus creating a Blue Ocean.

Four Actions Framework (Eliminate-Reduce-Raise-Create Grid)

This framework guides companies in systematically creating value innovation by working through four key questions:

1. **Eliminate**: Which factors that the industry takes for granted should be eliminated?

2. **Reduce**: Which factors should be reduced well below the industry's standard?

3. **Raise**: Which factors should be raised well above the industry's standard?

4. **Create**: Which factors should be created that the industry has never offered?

Six Paths Framework

The Six Paths Framework allows companies to break out of the accepted boundaries of competition and reconstruct market realities to create Blue Oceans. The six paths are:

1. Look across alternative industries.

2. Look across strategic groups within industries.

3. Look across the chain of buyers.

4. Look across complementary product and service offerings.

5. Look across functional or emotional appeal to buyers.

6. Look across time.

Practical Application and Benefits

Using these strategic tools, businesses can systematically explore new market spaces and create value innovation. This approach not only helps in identifying new opportunities but also provides a structured method for implementing innovative strategies that are sustainable and difficult for competitors to imitate.

Implementation of Blue Ocean Strategy

Successfully implementing the strategy involves several steps and overcoming organizational hurdles. Here's a step-by-step guide to creating your own:

1. **Visual Awakening**: Compare your business with competitors by drawing a strategy canvas. See where your strategy needs to change.

2. **Visual Exploration**: Go into the field to explore the six paths framework. Observe the distinctive advantages of alternative products and services.

3. **Visual Strategy Fair**: Draw your "to be" strategy canvas based on insights from field observations. Get feedback from customers, competitors' customers, and non-customers.

4. **Visual Communication**: Distribute the "before" and "after" strategy canvases to your organization to ensure everyone understands and is aligned with the new strategy.

Overcoming Organizational Hurdles

1. **Cognitive Hurdles**: Educate the organization about the need for change and the benefits of the new strategy.

2. **Resource Hurdles**: Focus on hotspots and allocate resources to areas that are critical to the new strategy.

3. **Motivational Hurdles**: Inspire and engage employees by showing them the direct impact of the new strategy on the company's success.

4. **Political Hurdles**: Address opposition by identifying and tackling potential obstacles and securing key allies.

Building a Supportive Culture for Innovation

Creating a culture that supports innovation is crucial for the successful implementation of Blue Ocean Strategy. This involves fostering an environment where creativity is encouraged, failure is seen as a learning opportunity, and employees are empowered to take initiative and experiment with new ideas.

Challenges and Risks

While Blue Ocean Strategy offers a powerful approach to business innovation, it is not without challenges and risks. Companies must be aware of potential obstacles and develop strategies to mitigate them.

Potential Obstacles

1. **Market Uncertainty**: Creating a new market space involves uncertainty and risk. There is no guarantee that the new market will be successful.

2. **Organizational Resistance**: Employees and managers may resist change, especially if they are accustomed to traditional ways of competing.

3. **Resource Allocation**: Developing a Blue Ocean Strategy may require significant investment in terms of time, money, and resources.

Managing Risk and Uncertainty

1. **Pilot Projects**: Start with small-scale pilot projects to test new ideas and reduce risk.

2. **Customer Feedback**: Continuously gather and analyze customer feedback to refine and improve the new offering.

3. **Flexible Approach**: Be prepared to pivot and adjust the strategy based on market response and emerging trends.

Strategies for Sustained Innovation and Competitive Advantage

1. **Continuous Improvement**: Regularly review and update the strategy to ensure it remains relevant and effective.

2. **Innovation Culture**: Foster a culture of continuous innovation where employees are encouraged to think creatively and challenge the status quo.

3. **Collaboration**: Collaborate with external partners, such as startups, research institutions, and industry experts, to bring in fresh perspectives and ideas.

More Case Studies and Real-World Examples

Several companies have successfully applied Blue Ocean Strategy to create new market spaces and achieve significant growth. Here are a few in-depth examples:

Apple's iTunes

- **Background**: Before iTunes, the music industry was dominated by physical CD sales, and digital music was plagued by piracy.

- **Blue Ocean Strategy**: Apple created iTunes, a digital platform that offered a legal, easy-to-use, and affordable way to purchase and download music.

- **Outcome**: iTunes revolutionized the music industry, creating a new market for digital music and making Apple a dominant player in the industry.

Southwest Airlines

- **Background**: The airline industry was characterized by high costs and intense competition.

- **Blue Ocean Strategy**: Southwest Airlines focused on offering low-cost, point-to-point flights with no frills, targeting price-sensitive customers who previously traveled by car or bus.

- **Outcome**: Southwest Airlines created a new market space within the airline industry and became one of the most profitable airlines in the world.

Starbucks

- **Background**: Before Starbucks, coffee was a commodity product, and coffee shops were mostly utilitarian.

- **Blue Ocean Strategy**: Starbucks created a new market by offering a unique customer experience with high-quality coffee, comfortable ambiance, and friendly service.

- **Outcome**: Starbucks transformed coffee drinking into a social experience and established itself as a global brand.

Summary

In today's dynamic and competitive business environment, innovation is crucial for survival and growth. Blue Ocean Strategy offers a powerful framework for creating new market spaces and achieving value innovation. By focusing on creating uncontested market space and making the competition irrelevant, businesses can unlock new opportunities and achieve sustainable growth.

As we have seen from the various examples and case studies, companies that successfully implement Blue Ocean Strategy can achieve significant competitive advantages and transform their industries. However, it requires a strategic approach, a supportive culture, and the ability to overcome organizational hurdles.

In conclusion, businesses that embrace Blue Ocean Strategy and continuously seek to innovate will be better positioned to thrive in the ever-changing marketplace. The future of business innovation lies in the ability to create new market spaces and deliver exceptional value to customers.

Chapter 5

Leveraging Technology for Acceleration

"The best way to predict the future is to invent it."

— Alan Kay

It is clear that technology has become an indispensable tool for businesses in the aesthetic industry. From streamlining operations to enhancing patient care, technology offers numerous benefits for cosmetic surgeons and medical spa owners looking to optimize their practices. Let's delve deeper into how you can leverage technology to achieve these goals and take your practice to new heights.

Selecting the Right Technological Tools

The first step in leveraging technology for your practice is selecting the right tools to meet your specific needs. Two essential systems to consider are electronic health records (EHR) and client relationship management (CRM) systems.

Electronic Health Records (EHR) System:

An EHR system is essential for modern medical practices as it digitizes patient records, improves accessibility, and enhances patient safety. With an EHR system, you can eliminate the need for manual notetaking and record-keeping, reducing errors and improving efficiency. Additionally, EHR systems offer features such as appointment scheduling, medication management, and lab integration, allowing for seamless coordination of patient care.

Actionable Advice: When selecting an EHR system for your practice, consider factors such as ease of use, interoperability with other systems, and compliance with regulatory standards such as HIPAA. Take advantage of free trials or demos to test different systems and determine which one best fits your practice's workflow and needs.

Real-Life Example: Dr. Smith's Plastic Surgery Clinic implemented an EHR system that allowed staff to access patient records securely from any location. The system streamlined appointment scheduling, reduced administrative workload, and improved patient satisfaction by providing quicker access to medical information.

Client Relationship Management (CRM) System:

A CRM system helps you manage interactions with current and potential clients, from initial contact to post-treatment follow-up. CRM systems centralize client information, track communication history, and automate marketing campaigns, allowing for more personalized and effective engagement. By leveraging a CRM system, you can enhance client relationships, increase retention rates, and drive business growth.

Actionable Advice: Look for a CRM system that integrates seamlessly with your EHR system to ensure smooth communication and data sharing between platforms. Customize your CRM system to track key metrics such as client demographics, treatment history, and appointment preferences. Use automated workflows and email marketing features to nurture client relationships and encourage repeat visits.

Real-Life Example: Dr. Johnson's Medical Spa implemented a CRM system that automated appointment reminders and follow-up emails to clients. The system tracked client preferences and treatment history, allowing staff to personalize recommendations and improve the overall client experience.

Automating Repetitive Tasks and Streamlining Workflows

Once you have the right technological tools in place, the next step is to automate repetitive tasks and streamline workflows to improve efficiency and productivity.

Appointment Scheduling Software:

Appointment scheduling software allows clients to book appointments online, reducing the need for manual booking and streamlining the appointment process. By automating appointment reminders and confirmations, you can minimize no-shows and optimize your schedule for maximum efficiency.

Actionable Advice: Choose appointment scheduling software that integrates with your EHR and CRM systems to ensure seamless communication and data synchronization. Customize your scheduling system to accommodate different appointment types, providers, and availability. Provide clients with self-service options to reschedule or cancel appointments online to reduce administrative burden.

Real-Life Example: Dr. Garcia's Dermatology Clinic implemented appointment scheduling software that allowed clients to book appointments directly through the clinic's website. The software automatically sent appointment reminders and confirmations via email and text message, reducing no-show rates and improving overall appointment efficiency.

Embracing Telemedicine and Virtual Consultations

In recent years, telemedicine and virtual consultations have gained popularity as convenient and accessible alternatives to traditional in-person visits. By embracing these technologies, you can expand your reach, improve accessibility, and provide more flexible care options for your clients.

Telemedicine: Telemedicine refers to the use of technology to deliver remote healthcare services, such as virtual consultations, follow-ups, and post-operative care. With telemedicine, clients can receive expert advice and treatment recommendations from the comfort of their homes, eliminating the need for travel and reducing wait times.

Actionable Advice: Invest in secure video conferencing software that complies with privacy regulations to ensure the confidentiality of virtual consultations. Train your staff on telemedicine best practices, including conducting virtual assessments, documenting patient encounters, and providing remote care instructions. Offer flexible scheduling options for telemedicine appointments to accommodate clients' busy schedules.

Real-Life Example: Dr. Martinez's Plastic Surgery Practice implemented a telemedicine platform that allowed clients to schedule virtual consultations and follow-ups. The platform facilitated real-time video conferencing with clients, enabling personalized assessments and treatment planning without the need for in-person visits.

Incorporating Advanced Imaging Technology

Advanced imaging technology, such as 3D scanning and simulation software, can enhance patient consultations and improve communication between providers and clients. By providing clients with realistic previews of their desired outcomes, you can manage expectations, build trust, and increase client satisfaction.

Actionable Advice: Invest in training for your staff to ensure they can effectively utilize advanced imaging technology during patient consultations. Customize simulation software to provide personalized treatment recommendations and visualize potential outcomes for different procedures. Incorporate advanced imaging technology into your marketing efforts to showcase your expertise and attract new clients.

Real-Life Example: Dr. Kim's Cosmetic Surgery Center invested in 3D scanning technology that allowed clients to visualize potential outcomes of cosmetic procedures before undergoing treatment. The technology improved client understanding and satisfaction, leading to higher conversion rates and positive reviews.

In conclusion, leveraging technology is essential for cosmetic surgeons and medical spa owners looking to optimize their practices and deliver exceptional care to their clients. By selecting the right technological tools, automating repetitive tasks, embracing telemedicine and virtual consultations, and incorporating advanced imaging technology, practitioners can enhance efficiency, improve patient experiences, and achieve sustainable growth and success in the competitive aesthetic industry.

Some of the latest advancements in aesthetic medicine include:

1. **Energy-Based Devices:** Energy-based devices use various forms of energy, such as laser, radiofrequency, ultrasound, and microneedling, to rejuvenate the skin, reduce wrinkles, tighten sagging skin, and improve overall skin texture. These devices are continually being refined and upgraded to deliver more precise and effective results with minimal downtime.

2. **Platelet-Rich Plasma (PRP) Therapy:** PRP therapy involves extracting a patient's own blood, separating the platelets, and injecting the concentrated platelet-rich plasma into targeted areas of the skin to stimulate collagen production, promote tissue regeneration, and improve skin tone and texture. Advanced PRP delivery systems and techniques are continually being developed to optimize outcomes and enhance patient satisfaction.

3. **Microfocused Ultrasound (MFU) Devices:** MFU devices deliver focused ultrasound energy deep into the skin to stimulate collagen production and tighten the underlying tissues, resulting in a lifting and

firming effect. These devices are particularly effective for non-surgical facelifts, neck lifts, and body contouring procedures.

4. **High-Intensity Focused Ultrasound (HIFU):** HIFU technology utilizes focused ultrasound energy to target and heat specific layers of tissue beneath the skin, triggering collagen remodeling and tissue tightening. HIFU treatments are commonly used for facial rejuvenation, skin tightening, and body contouring, with advancements in technology allowing for more precise and customizable treatments.

5. **Cryolipolysis (Fat Freezing):** Cryolipolysis is a non-invasive fat reduction technique that uses controlled cooling to freeze and destroy fat cells, which are then naturally eliminated from the body over time. Newer cryolipolysis devices offer improved cooling technology and applicator designs to enhance patient comfort and optimize results.

6. **Fractional Laser Technology:** Fractional laser technology delivers laser energy in a fractionated pattern to create microscopic treatment zones in the skin, stimulating collagen production and promoting skin resurfacing and rejuvenation. Recent advancements in fractional laser technology include improved precision, reduced downtime, and enhanced safety profiles.

7. **Injectable Fillers and Neurotoxins:** Injectable fillers, such as hyaluronic acid-based fillers and collagen-stimulating fillers, continue to evolve with new formulations and delivery methods that provide longer-lasting results and more natural-looking outcomes. Similarly, neurotoxins like Botox and Dysport are being refined to offer more precise and customizable treatments with fewer side effects.

8. **Regenerative Medicine:** Regenerative medicine techniques, including stem cell therapy, growth factor treatments, and tissue engineering, are gaining popularity in aesthetic medicine for their potential to enhance tissue regeneration, promote healing, and improve overall skin quality.

These innovative treatments harness the body's natural healing processes to address various aesthetic concerns.

9. **Augmented Reality (AR) and Virtual Reality (VR) Technology:** AR and VR technology are being used to simulate cosmetic procedures and visualize potential outcomes before treatment, allowing patients to make more informed decisions and feel confident about their choices. These immersive technologies also enhance patient education and engagement, leading to higher satisfaction rates.

10. **Personalized Skincare and DNA Testing:** Advances in genetics and personalized medicine have led to the development of skincare products and treatments tailored to individual genetic profiles and skin characteristics. DNA testing can identify specific skin concerns and genetic predispositions, allowing practitioners to customize skincare regimens and treatment plans for optimal results.

Niching Down

Chapter 6

Niche: Expertise Through Specialization

"Expertise is knowing more and more about less and less."

— Nicholas M. Butler

Focusing on a specific niche can significantly elevate your position as an expert in that area, offering numerous advantages that establish your authority, build a loyal audience, and create a sustainable business model. This expanded exploration delves deeper into the various facets of how concentrating on a niche can position you as an expert.

Deep Knowledge and Expertise

In-Depth Understanding

By honing in on a niche, you develop a profound understanding of that particular field. This allows you to dive deep into the subject matter, learning all its nuances and complexities. Such depth of knowledge sets you apart from generalists and enhances your credibility as an expert. The more specialized your knowledge, the more valuable your insights become to those seeking expertise in that area. For instance, a financial advisor focusing solely on retirement planning can offer more precise and tailored advice than a general financial advisor, making them more attractive to clients in that stage of life.

The importance of positioning in the minds of consumers is emphasized in the classic marketing book *Positioning: The Battle for*

Your Mind by Al Ries and Jack Trout[4]. It highlights how being a specialist can help a brand stand out and attract a dedicated customer base. Seth Godin, in *Purple Cow*[5], also discusses the concept of being remarkable in a crowded market and how specializing can make a business stand out and be more attractive to customers.

Continuous Learning

Specializing in a niche encourages continuous learning, ensuring that your knowledge remains current and authoritative. This ongoing education is crucial for maintaining your expert status. For example, a tech blogger specializing in artificial intelligence (AI) must keep abreast of the latest advancements and trends in AI, allowing them to provide timely and relevant information to their audience . This commitment to staying updated helps reinforce your authority in your chosen niche.

Targeted Audience

Identifying Specific Needs

When you focus on a niche, you can better identify and address the specific needs and pain points of a targeted audience. Understanding their unique challenges allows you to tailor your content, products, and services to meet their exact requirements, demonstrating your expertise and understanding. For instance, a nutritionist specializing in vegan diets can provide more relevant meal plans, recipes, and nutritional advice than a general nutritionist, directly addressing the concerns of vegan clients .

Building a Loyal Following

---

4 Ries, Al, and Jack Trout. *Positioning: The Battle for Your Mind*. McGraw-Hill, 2001.

5 Godin, Seth. *Purple Cow: Transform Your Business by Being Remarkable*. Portfolio, 2003.

This targeted approach attracts an audience highly interested in that particular subject, leading to increased engagement and loyalty. Your focused audience is more likely to trust your insights and become loyal followers or customers. When your expertise aligns closely with their needs, they perceive you as a trusted advisor who truly understands their specific issues. This loyalty translates into sustained engagement and word-of-mouth referrals, further establishing your reputation as an expert.

Strong Brand Identity

Distinctive Positioning

Specializing in a niche helps you create a distinctive brand identity. Your expertise in a specific area sets you apart from competitors, making it easier for your audience to recognize and remember you as a go-to expert in that field. For example, Neil Patel's focus on digital marketing and SEO has made his brand synonymous with those topics. His distinct positioning as an SEO expert has helped him build a strong, recognizable brand .

Consistent Messaging

Consistent messaging across all your marketing channels reinforces your expertise and builds a strong, cohesive brand that resonates with your target audience. By delivering clear, consistent messages that align with your niche, you ensure that your brand remains top-of-mind for your audience. This consistency helps in building trust and recognition, making it easier for people to associate you with your area of specialization.

Enhanced Credibility and Trust

Authority Building

Being highly knowledgeable in a specific area helps establish your authority. When people see that you consistently provide valuable insights and solutions related to your niche, they are more likely to trust your expertise. For instance, Dave Ramsey's focus on personal finance and debt management has established him as a trusted authority in that field, leading to a vast following and numerous speaking engagements .

Media and Speaking Opportunities

This trust is further reinforced by media and speaking opportunities, as journalists, event organizers, and industry leaders often seek out specialists for their insights and commentary. These opportunities enhance your credibility and visibility, positioning you as a trusted expert in your field. For example, Marie Kondo's specialization in decluttering and organizing led to media appearances, a bestselling book, and a popular Netflix series, significantly boosting her credibility and reach .

Effective Marketing and SEO

Targeted Content

Creating content that addresses specific niche topics can improve your search engine rankings. When your content is highly relevant to a specific audience, it is more likely to be found by people searching for that information, increasing your online visibility. For instance, a blog focused solely on gluten-free baking will attract a dedicated readership looking for those specific recipes, helping it rank higher in related search queries.

Keyword Optimization

Focusing on niche-specific keywords helps you rank higher in search engine results for those terms, driving more organic traffic from users interested in your specific area of expertise. This targeted SEO strategy enhances your online presence and authority. By consistently using relevant keywords and optimizing your content, you increase the likelihood of appearing in search results, attracting a more focused and engaged audience.

Community Engagement

Building Relationships

Engaging with a niche community allows you to build strong relationships with your audience. Participating in niche forums, social media groups, and industry events helps you connect with like-minded individuals and establish yourself as a trusted community member. For example, a fitness trainer specializing in high-intensity interval training (HIIT) might join and contribute to HIIT-focused online communities, sharing tips and advice, and thus building a strong network of followers .

Providing Value

By offering valuable content, advice, and solutions tailored to your niche audience, you demonstrate your commitment to their needs. This value provision fosters trust and positions you as an indispensable resource within the community. Regularly contributing valuable insights and engaging with your audience reinforces your role as an expert and helps build a loyal following.

Higher Conversion Rates

Tailored Offerings

When your products or services are specifically designed to address the needs of your niche, they are more likely to resonate with your audience. This tailored approach increases the likelihood of conversions, as potential customers see the direct relevance and benefits of what you offer. For instance, a SaaS company that provides specialized software solutions for dental practices will likely see higher conversion rates compared to a general software provider, as their offering is precisely what the target audience needs .

Customer Loyalty

Satisfied niche customers are more likely to become repeat buyers and refer others to you, creating a loyal customer base. Their loyalty stems from the perceived value and expertise you provide within the specific niche, driving higher conversion rates and business success. When customers feel understood and valued, they are more likely to remain loyal and advocate for your brand, enhancing your reputation and reach.

Competitive Advantage

Less Competition

Focusing on a niche often means facing less competition compared to broader markets. By concentrating on a specific area, you can dominate that niche and become the leading expert, enjoying a larger share of the market. This competitive edge allows you to stand out more easily and attract a dedicated audience looking for specialized knowledge and solutions.

Barriers to Entry

Your in-depth knowledge and established reputation in a niche create barriers to entry for new competitors, who will find it challenging to match your level of expertise and audience loyalty. This competitive advantage ensures your continued success and authority in your chosen field. By maintaining a high standard of knowledge and service, you can deter potential competitors and solidify your position as a niche leader.

Business Growth and Innovation

Focused Innovation

Concentrating on a niche allows you to innovate specifically for that market. You can develop new products, services, or solutions that cater directly to the unique needs of your niche audience, driving business growth. For example, a company specializing in eco-friendly packaging solutions can continuously innovate within that niche, addressing evolving environmental concerns and customer demands .

Scalability

Once you establish yourself as an expert in one niche, you can replicate your success in related niches, expanding your business while maintaining a strong foundation of expertise. This scalability enables sustainable growth and innovation, reinforcing your position as a leader in your chosen field. By leveraging your expertise in one niche, you can explore adjacent markets and broaden your influence and revenue streams.

Case Studies: The Power of Niching Down

Apple Inc.: Innovation Through Specialized Talent

Apple Inc. offers a prime example of the power of focusing on a niche, particularly in the realm of design and user experience. Steve Jobs' emphasis on recruiting and retaining top talent who shared his vision for innovation and excellence helped Apple create groundbreaking products. The company's focus on delivering premium, user-friendly technology products, such as the iPhone and MacBook, revolutionized the tech industry. By zeroing in on this niche, Apple established itself as a leader and innovator, demonstrating how specialized focus can drive unparalleled success .

Neil Patel: SEO and Digital Marketing Expertise

Neil Patel, a prominent figure in digital marketing, exemplifies the benefits of niche specialization. By concentrating on SEO and online marketing, Patel has built a robust brand recognized globally. His targeted content, consistent messaging, and deep expertise have made him a sought-after consultant and speaker in the digital marketing space. His success underscores the importance of deep knowledge and targeted focus in establishing oneself as an industry authority .

Marie Kondo: The Art of Tidying

Marie Kondo's specialization in decluttering and organizing has turned her into a global phenomenon. Her unique approach to tidying, encapsulated in the KonMari Method[6], resonated deeply with audiences worldwide. Her books, media appearances, and Netflix series have positioned her as the ultimate authority on decluttering. Kondo's rise to prominence highlights how focusing on a specific niche can lead to widespread recognition and influence .

---

[6] Kondo, Marie. *The Life-Changing Magic of Tidying Up: The Japanese Art of Decluttering and Organizing*. Ten Speed Press, 2014.

Conclusion

Focusing on a specific niche positions you as an expert by enabling deep knowledge, attracting a targeted audience, building a strong brand, and enhancing credibility. It also facilitates effective marketing, community engagement, and higher conversion rates. The competitive advantages and opportunities for innovation and growth further solidify your standing as a leader in your niche. By committing to a niche, you create a sustainable and authoritative presence that distinguishes you from generalists and drives long-term success. This targeted approach ensures that you are recognized as a valuable and trusted expert, capable of providing specialized solutions and insights that meet the unique needs of your audience.

By understanding and implementing the principles of niche specialization, you can build a successful and influential career or business. The benefits of this focused approach are clear: deeper knowledge, stronger relationships, higher credibility, and sustained growth. Embracing a niche is not just about limiting your scope; it's about amplifying your impact and establishing a legacy of expertise and excellence.

FINESSE

Exceptional Customer Service

Chapter 7

Enhancing the Patient & Guest Experience

"You've got to start with the customer experience and work back toward the technology, not the other way around."

— Steve Jobs

Designing an Exceptional Journey in Cosmetic Surgery and Medical Spa Settings

In the world of cosmetic surgery and medical spas, providing an exceptional patient experience is not just a goal but a necessity. It's the cornerstone upon which successful practices are built, and it's what sets apart the exceptional from the merely adequate. Crafting an unparalleled experience for each patient requires a combination of skill, dedication, and a deep understanding of their needs and desires.

Creating a Welcoming and Comfortable Environment

Picture this: a patient walks into your facility, nervous yet hopeful for the transformation they seek. What do they encounter? A sterile, impersonal environment? Or a warm, inviting space that immediately puts them at ease? The latter is what sets exceptional practices apart.

From the moment patients step through the door, every detail matters. The ambiance, the decor, the cleanliness—these elements contribute to their overall experience. A welcoming environment not only calms nerves but also sets the stage for trust and connection.

Take, for example, Dr. Smith's Medical Spa. Dr. Smith understands that the journey begins the moment a patient enters the door. With soothing colors, comfortable furnishings, and a focus on cleanliness, patients immediately feel at home. The receptionist greets them by name, offering a genuine smile and reassurance. It's these small touches that make all the difference.

Effective Communication: The Foundation of Trust

In any relationship, communication is key. This holds especially true in the patient-provider dynamic. Patients come to cosmetic surgeons and medical spas with a myriad of concerns and expectations. It's crucial to listen actively, without interruption or judgment, to truly understand their needs.

Dr. Patel, a renowned cosmetic surgeon, emphasizes the importance of active listening. "So many of my stellar patient reviews have commented on the quality of my listening," says Dr. Patel. "If they feel truly heard, they will connect with you and trust you."

Clear, honest communication about procedures, risks, and expected outcomes is paramount. Patients should feel informed and empowered to make decisions that align with their goals. By building trust through effective communication, providers can ensure patient satisfaction and long-term loyalty.

Personalized Treatment Plans: Tailoring Care to Individual Needs

No two patients are alike, and neither are their aesthetic goals. Exceptional practices understand this and embrace a personalized approach to care. Rather than offering one-size-fits-all solutions, they tailor treatment plans to each patient's unique needs and desires.

Dr. Nguyen, a leading cosmetic surgeon, explains, "People see through cookie-cutter offerings as inferior. By customizing treatment plans based on individual goals and medical history, we provide a truly personalized experience."

This may involve offering a range of treatment options, explaining the pros and cons of each, and guiding patients towards the most suitable choice. By involving patients in the decision-making process, providers empower them to take ownership of their journey.

Embracing Technological Advancements: Innovating for Excellence

In today's fast-paced world, technology is constantly evolving. Exceptional practices stay ahead of the curve by investing in the latest advancements and staying up-to-date with industry trends. Patients expect state-of-the-art facilities and cutting-edge treatments that deliver exceptional results.

Dr. Rodriguez, a pioneer in medical aesthetics, understands the importance of innovation. "You don't have to break the bank with every new gadget," says Dr. Rodriguez. "But investing in modern equipment and offering the latest treatments ensures that we're providing the best possible care for our patients."

Whether it's laser technology for skin rejuvenation or advanced imaging systems for precise surgical planning, embracing technological advancements enhances the patient experience and sets practices apart from the competition.

Post-Treatment Care and Follow-Up: Building Lasting Relationships

The journey doesn't end once the treatment is complete. Exceptional practices understand the importance of post-treatment care and follow-up in ensuring patient satisfaction and fostering long-term relationships.

Dr. Lee, a dedicated medical spa owner, emphasizes the value of post-treatment support. "Nobody wants to feel like you abandoned them once you got their money," says Dr. Lee. "Regular follow-up calls, post-treatment check-ups, and personalized aftercare instructions show patients that we're with them every step of the way."

By providing ongoing support and guidance, practices demonstrate their commitment to patient well-being beyond the procedure. This not only enhances satisfaction but also encourages positive word-of-mouth referrals, driving growth and success.

Providing Outstanding Customer Service: Building Loyalty Beyond Expectations

In the realm of cosmetic surgery and medical spas, clients are not just patients—they're valued customers seeking a premium experience. Exceptional practices go above and beyond to deliver outstanding customer service that exceeds expectations.

Tactical Empathy: Connecting on a Deeper Level

At the core of exceptional customer service lies tactical empathy—an ability to connect with clients on a deeper level and understand their needs and concerns. By actively listening and responding with empathy and understanding, providers can foster trust and loyalty.

Dr. Garcia, a seasoned cosmetic surgeon, teaches his team the importance of tactical empathy. "It's crucial to listen attentively to your clients' needs and concerns," says Dr. Garcia. "By establishing clear lines of communication, you can ensure that your clients feel heard and valued."

Going the Extra Mile: Exceeding Expectations

Exceptional practices don't just meet expectations—they exceed them. By offering personalized recommendations, tailoring treatments to individual needs, and providing unexpected perks or incentives, they create memorable experiences that leave a lasting impression.

Dr. Martinez, a passionate medical spa owner, believes in the power of going the extra mile. "Give things away for free. Be generous," says Dr. Martinez. "Always look to deliver more than expected, and you will never fail."

Building Client Loyalty: Nurturing Relationships

Client loyalty is the lifeblood of any successful practice. Exceptional practices cultivate a nurturing environment where clients feel valued and appreciated. From warm greetings to personalized service, every interaction reinforces the bond between provider and client.

Dr. Kim, a dedicated cosmetic surgeon, emphasizes the importance of nurturing relationships. "Train your staff to greet clients warmly, address them by name, and offer a friendly and professional demeanor at all times," says Dr. Kim. "It's these small gestures that build trust and loyalty."

Encouraging Referrals: Harnessing the Power of Word-of-Mouth

Satisfied clients are not just loyal—they're advocates. Exceptional practices leverage the power of positive word-of-mouth by encouraging referrals and incentivizing clients to share their experiences with others.

Implementing a referral program, asking for testimonials, or simply requesting a favor of a referral can all contribute to a steady stream of new clients. By harnessing the power of word-of-mouth, practices can expand their reach and grow their client base organically.

Always Aiming to Give and Serve as Much as Possible: The Heart of Success

Beyond the strategies and techniques lies a fundamental principle: the desire to give and serve as much as possible. Exceptional practices are driven by a commitment to service, empathy, and making a positive impact on the lives of others.

Dr. Thompson, a visionary cosmetic surgeon, believes in the power of service. "At the heart of every successful aesthetic practice lies the desire to give and serve as much as possible," says Dr. Thompson. "Generosity attracts revenue like nothing else."

Investing in Community: Making a Difference Beyond the Clinic

Finally, exceptional practices look beyond their walls and invest in their communities. Whether through philanthropic endeavors, pro bono services, or volunteer work, they seek to make a positive impact on the world around them.

Dr. Rodriguez, a compassionate medical spa owner, understands the importance of giving back. "By investing our time and expertise in charitable initiatives, we not only make a difference in the lives of others but also showcase the quality of our character," says Dr. Rodriguez.

Managing and Resolving Patient Complaints: Turning Challenges into Opportunities

Inevitably, challenges will arise. Whether it's a patient complaint or a difficult situation, exceptional practices approach these obstacles with professionalism and grace.

Establishing a culture of open communication is key. Encouraging staff to actively listen to patients' concerns and respond promptly and empathetically sets the stage for resolution. By acknowledging concerns, conducting thorough investigations, and offering realistic solutions, practices can turn negative experiences into positive outcomes.

Dr. Chang, a seasoned cosmetic surgeon, believes in the power of proactive resolution. "By implementing a comprehensive feedback system and addressing concerns promptly, we not only minimize the risk of negative reviews but also demonstrate our commitment to patient satisfaction," says Dr. Chang.

In conclusion, designing an exceptional patient experience in the realm of cosmetic surgery and medical spas requires a holistic approach that encompasses every aspect of the patient journey. From creating a welcoming environment to providing outstanding customer service, investing in community, and effectively managing challenges, exceptional practices set themselves apart and ensure long-term success. By prioritizing service, empathy, and innovation, they not only transform lives but also leave a lasting legacy in the field of aesthetics.

Chapter 8

Insights from Hospitality

"The true meaning of hospitality is when people leave feeling better about themselves, not better about the place they were in."

— *Danny Meyer*

"The Heart of Hospitality"

Aesthetic practices, day spa, and med spas all have a lot in common with hotels and other hospitality businesses. I actually learned a great deal about enhancing guest experiences from well-know hotel groups who do it right. "The Heart of Hospitality"[7] by Micah Solomon is a definitive guide on how to create and maintain an outstanding guest experience in the hospitality industry. Drawing on the wisdom of industry leaders and the practices of successful hoteliers, the book provides a comprehensive roadmap for achieving service excellence. The key strategies detailed in the book encompass personalization, attention to detail, employee empowerment, consistency, emotional connections, proactive service, innovation, complaint handling, training and development, leadership and culture, and feedback and improvement.

After reading this book, I outlined how the insights could be applied to my businesses and instantly went to work implementing many of the nuggets of advice to both my clinical practice and spa.

---

[7] Solomon, Micah. *The Heart of Hospitality: Great Hotel and Restaurant Leaders Share Their Secrets*. Select Books, Inc., 2016.

1. Personalization

Personalization is central to creating a memorable guest experience. It involves customizing services to meet the individual preferences and needs of each guest. This could range from remembering a guest's favorite room setup to noting their preferred dining options.

Examples:

- **Ritz-Carlton**: I've referred to the Ritz already in the chapter discussing staff empowerment. The Ritz-Carlton is also renowned for its personalized service. Staff members are trained to note guest preferences and details during their stay. For instance, if a guest mentions they like a particular type of pillow, this preference is recorded and honored in future stays, ensuring a personalized experience.

- **Fairmont Hotels & Resorts**: Fairmont's "Fairmont Fit" program provides personalized fitness gear and equipment directly to guests' rooms. By tailoring services to individual fitness routines, Fairmont enhances guest satisfaction and convenience.

2. Attention to Detail

Attention to detail involves meticulous attention to every aspect of the guest experience, from the cleanliness of the rooms to the quality of amenities provided. Small touches can have a significant impact on guest satisfaction.

Examples:

- **Four Seasons Hotels**: The Four Seasons is known for its impeccable attention to detail. From ensuring rooms are spotless to providing luxury toiletries and carefully chosen in-room amenities, the hotel chain goes above and beyond to create a refined experience.

- **Aman Resorts**: Aman Resorts focus on creating a serene and harmonious environment. This includes everything from the architectural design of their properties to the selection of in-room scents and the presentation of meals, all meticulously planned to enhance the guest experience.

3. Empowering Employees

As mentioned before, empowering employees means giving them the authority and resources to solve problems and make decisions that enhance the guest experience. This empowerment leads to quicker resolutions and more personalized service.

Examples:

- **Nordstrom**: Although not a hotel, Nordstrom's approach to employee empowerment is exemplary. Employees are encouraged to use their judgment to resolve customer issues, resulting in a reputation for excellent service.

- **The Ritz-Carlton**: Employees at The Ritz-Carlton are empowered with a discretionary budget to resolve guest issues on the spot, without needing managerial approval. This autonomy allows staff to address and rectify issues swiftly, enhancing guest satisfaction.

4. Consistency

Consistency in service delivery is crucial for building trust and reliability. Guests expect a uniform level of service across all touchpoints, whether they are visiting a hotel for the first time or returning for the tenth.

Examples:

- **Marriott International**: Marriott maintains strict standards across its properties to ensure consistency in service. Guests can expect the same level of cleanliness, quality of amenities, and customer service regardless of the location.

- **Starbucks**: Similar to Marriott, Starbucks offers a consistent experience across all its stores. From the taste of the coffee to the ambiance and customer service, the brand ensures that guests receive the same experience worldwide.

5. Creating Emotional Connections

Building emotional connections with guests involves creating genuine, memorable interactions that go beyond transactional exchanges. These connections foster loyalty and repeat business.

Examples:

- **Kimpton Hotels**: Kimpton encourages its staff to engage with guests on a personal level, remembering names, and preferences, and celebrating special occasions. This personal touch helps build strong emotional connections.

- **Disney Resorts**: Disney excels in creating magical experiences that resonate emotionally with guests. From character interactions to personalized greetings, Disney creates an emotional bond that keeps guests returning.

6. Proactive Service

Proactive service means anticipating guest needs and addressing them before they arise. This approach involves observing guest behaviors and preferences and acting on them without waiting for a request.

Examples:

- **Mandarin Oriental**: Staff at Mandarin Oriental are trained to anticipate guest needs. For instance, if a guest orders room service breakfast for several days, the staff may proactively offer to set up a standing order for the duration of the stay.

- **Singapore Airlines**: Known for its exceptional service, Singapore Airlines' cabin crew are trained to anticipate passenger needs, such as offering a drink before it's requested or providing blankets when passengers appear cold.

7. Innovation

We've discussed innovation and technology for aesthetic practice. Likewise for hospitality, innovation involves continuously seeking new ways to improve the guest experience. This could involve adopting new technologies, offering unique experiences, or refining existing services.

Examples:

- **Hilton's Digital Key**: Hilton offers a digital key feature through its app, allowing guests to check-in, choose their room, and unlock their door using their smartphones. This innovation enhances convenience and streamlines the guest experience.

- **Marriott's Chatbots**: Marriott uses AI-powered chatbots to handle common guest inquiries and requests. This technology not only speeds up response times but also frees up staff to focus on more personalized service.

8. Handling Complaints Gracefully

Effective complaint handling is crucial for turning negative experiences into positive ones. It involves listening to guests, empathizing with their concerns, and resolving issues promptly and satisfactorily.

Examples:

- **Zappos**: Zappos, an online retailer known for its customer service, trains its staff to handle complaints with empathy and efficiency. The company's commitment to resolving issues promptly has earned it a loyal customer base.

- **Hyatt Hotels**: Hyatt encourages staff to listen carefully to guest complaints, apologize sincerely, and take immediate corrective actions. This approach ensures that guests feel heard and valued, even when things go wrong.

9. Training and Development

Investing in training and development for employees ensures they have the skills and knowledge needed to provide exceptional service. Continuous development opportunities help maintain high service standards and motivate staff.

Examples:

- **The Ritz-Carlton Leadership Center**: The Ritz-Carlton offers extensive training programs for its employees, focusing on service excellence and leadership development. These programs ensure that staff are well-equipped to deliver top-notch service.

- **Four Seasons' Continuous Training**: Four Seasons Hotels provide ongoing training and development opportunities for their staff, including workshops, e-learning modules, and mentorship programs. This commitment to employee growth translates to consistent, high-quality service for guests.

10. Leadership and Culture

Strong leadership and a positive organizational culture are fundamental to delivering outstanding guest experiences. Leaders should model exemplary behavior, inspire their teams, and foster a culture of service excellence.

Examples:

- **Virgin Group**: Richard Branson's leadership style at Virgin Group emphasizes employee empowerment and a fun, positive work environment. This culture of engagement and enthusiasm trickles down to the guest experience, creating a welcoming atmosphere.

- **The Ritz-Carlton's Gold Standards**: The Ritz-Carlton's Gold Standards, which include its credo, motto, and service values, form the foundation of its service culture. Leadership at all levels reinforces these standards, ensuring that every employee is committed to delivering exceptional service.

11. Feedback and Improvement

Actively seeking and utilizing guest feedback is vital for continuous improvement. Implementing systems to collect and analyze feedback helps identify areas for enhancement and demonstrates that guest opinions are valued.

Examples:

- **TripAdvisor Reviews**: Many hotels actively monitor and respond to TripAdvisor reviews, using the feedback to make necessary improvements and show guests that their opinions matter. Responding to reviews, both positive and negative, also helps build a rapport with guests.

- **Hyatt's Guest Surveys**: Hyatt Hotels utilize guest surveys to gather detailed feedback about their stay. The data collected is analyzed to identify trends and areas for improvement, ensuring that the hotel continuously enhances its services.

In a 2019 Southwest Hospitality Study, **more than three-fourths (77%)** of study respondents rated verbiage about a complimentary morning meal as their favorite phrase when considering booking a room in a hotel or resort. Even if they don't tear into box of cereal or 2-minute waffle, many travelers like knowing it's there—just in case.

The most important phrase for hotel or resort guests
is tied to the most important meal of the day
PREFERRED PHRASES MARKETERS USE TO COMMUNICATE WITH YOU ABOUT HOTELS OR RESORTS.

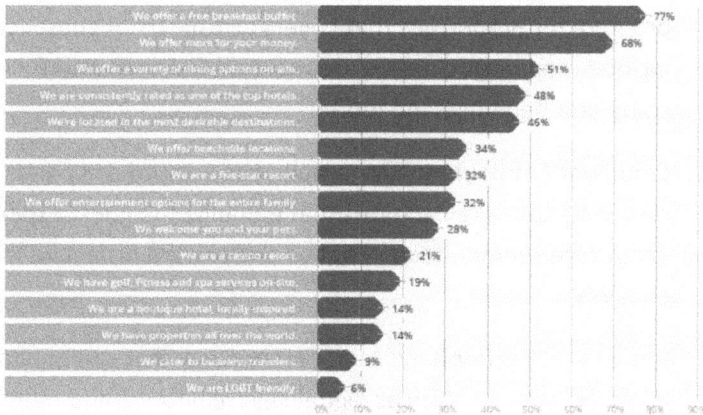

Figure 4. 77% overall chose "we offer a free breakfast buffet" as their preferred phrase.

A similar study for your specific practice environment could be extremely useful in designing your amenities or shaping your marketing materials.

Practical Implementation of Strategies

Implementing these strategies requires a structured approach and commitment from all levels of the organization. Here's a step-by-step guide to putting these principles into practice:

1. **Assess Current Practices**: Evaluate your current guest experience practices and identify areas for improvement.

Collect feedback from guests and employees to get a comprehensive view.

2. **Set Clear Goals**: Define what you want to achieve in terms of guest experience. Set measurable goals, such as improving guest satisfaction scores or increasing repeat business.

3. **Develop a Training Program**: Create a comprehensive training program for employees that covers all aspects of guest service. Include modules on personalization, attention to detail, complaint handling, and more.

4. **Empower Employees**: Give employees the authority and resources to make decisions that enhance the guest experience. Encourage them to take initiative and reward proactive behavior.

5. **Implement Technology**: Adopt technology that can enhance the guest experience, such as digital keys, chatbots, and mobile apps for personalized service.

6. **Monitor Consistency**: Regularly check that service standards are being met consistently across all touchpoints. Use mystery shoppers, guest surveys, and internal audits to monitor performance.

7. **Foster a Positive Culture**: Create a positive organizational culture that values service excellence. Recognize and reward employees who go above and beyond in delivering exceptional service.

8. **Encourage Feedback**: Implement systems to collect guest feedback, such as online reviews, surveys, and comment cards. Use this feedback to make continuous improvements.

9. **Lead by Example**: Ensure that leaders at all levels model the behavior they want to see in their teams. Provide ongoing

training and support to help leaders inspire and motivate their teams.

10. **Review and Adjust**: Regularly review your guest experience strategy and make adjustments based on feedback and changing guest expectations. Stay flexible and open to new ideas and innovations.

Summary

Enhancing the guest experience in the hospitality, as with any industry, requires a multi-faceted approach. By focusing on personalization, attention to detail, employee empowerment, consistency, emotional connections, proactive service, innovation, complaint handling, training and development, leadership and culture, and feedback and improvement, we can learn from hotels and other hospitality businesses to create memorable and exceptional experiences for our patients and guests. After that run-on sentence, are you as ready as I am to stay at a Ritz?

Self-Promotion

Chapter 9

Marketing and Branding to Win

"Your brand is what other people say about you when you're not in the room."

— Jeff Bezos

Crafting a Compelling Brand Identity

In today's competitive landscape, establishing a compelling brand identity is paramount for any business, especially in the aesthetics industry. Beyond merely having a logo or tagline, your brand encompasses the entirety of your practice's essence and the experiences it offers. As a business owner, it's essential to cultivate not only your practice's brand but also your personal brand. This is what resonates with potential clients, fostering trust and loyalty. Let's delve into the crucial elements of creating a compelling brand identity.

1.**Understanding Your Target Audience:**

Your brand should reflect your core values, goals, and the transformative experiences you offer. In the aesthetics industry, clients are not just looking for a service; they're seeking confidence, beauty, and self-assurance. By understanding your target audience, you can tailor your brand identity to resonate with their preferences, values, and aspirations.

An example of an audience-centric branding approach can be seen in Nike's marketing strategy, particularly with its campaign targeting female athletes. Nike recognized that women represented a significant and growing segment of the athletic apparel market but were often underserved and overlooked by traditional sports brands. In response, Nike launched the "Dream Crazier" campaign in 2019, which celebrated female athletes and challenged stereotypes and gender norms in sports.

Nike conducted extensive research to understand the needs, aspirations, and challenges of female athletes. They recognized that many women faced barriers and discrimination in sports, such as unequal pay, limited representation, and societal expectations regarding femininity and athleticism.

Based on their insights, Nike crafted a message that resonated with their audience's values and aspirations. The "Dream Crazier" campaign celebrated female athletes who defied expectations and pushed boundaries in their respective sports. The campaign highlighted stories of perseverance, resilience, and achievement, inspiring women to dream big and pursue their athletic goals.

They used powerful visuals and storytelling to convey its message. The campaign featured iconic athletes such as Serena Williams, Simone Biles, and Caster Semenya, showcasing their remarkable accomplishments and overcoming adversity. These stories were accompanied by stirring imagery and emotional narration, creating a powerful narrative that resonated with viewers.

Nike engaged with its audience through various channels, including social media, events, and collaborations. The brand encouraged women to share their own stories and experiences using the hashtag #DreamCrazier, fostering a sense of community and empowerment among female athletes worldwide.

The "Dream Crazier" campaign received widespread acclaim for its powerful message and impact. It sparked conversations about gender equality in sports and inspired women of all ages to pursue their athletic passions with confidence and determination. Nike's audience-centric approach not only strengthened its connection with female consumers but also positioned the brand as a champion of inclusivity and empowerment in sports.

2. Designing a Visually Appealing Brand Identity System:

Your logo, color palette, typography, and imagery should resonate with your target audience and convey your practice's personality and values.

First, you must understand your brand's mission, values, and unique selling proposition (USP). Clarify what sets your brand apart from competitors and its desired positioning in the market.

Then, you can generate a range of visual concepts and ideas that capture the essence of the brand. Experiment with typography, color palettes, imagery, and graphic elements to convey the brand's personality and values. Strive for simplicity and clarity in the design. Avoid unnecessary complexity and clutter that can dilute the brand's message. Ensure consistency in visual elements across all brand touchpoints to reinforce brand recognition and trust.

You can look to a Google search for ideas, but don't use a generic design that will undoubtedly contain some version of a lotus flower and say absolutely nothing about what sets your business apart.

Figure 5. Results of Google search: "good spa logo"

For more guidance, see *Designing Brand Identity: An Essential Guide for the Whole Branding Team* by Alina Wheeler. It provides a comprehensive overview of the branding process, including brand strategy, visual identity design, and brand implementation. It features real-world examples and best practices for creating effective brand identities.

3. Beyond Visual Elements:

Branding extends beyond visual elements—it permeates every aspect of your business. From the moment a client enters your practice to their post-treatment follow-up, every interaction shapes their perception of your brand.

Today more than ever, audiences crave authenticity. Be true to your brand's values and personality across all touchpoints. Consistency in messaging, visuals, and customer experience helps build trust and recognition.

4. Monitoring and Adaptation:

Keep a pulse on your online reputation, client feedback, and industry trends to adapt your brand messaging and visual identity accordingly.

One helpful tip is to set up Google Alerts for your name, brand, or relevant keywords. Google will send you email notifications whenever new content mentioning the specified keywords is indexed by the search engine.

Social media monitoring tools like Hootsuite, Buffer, or Sprout Social are available to track mentions of your brand across various social media platforms. These tools also allow you to monitor conversations, respond to comments, and analyze sentiment.

You or a member of your team should regularly monitor website analytics to track traffic sources, user engagement, and conversions. Pay attention to any changes in website traffic or user behavior that may indicate shifts in your online reputation.

Finally, Collect feedback from patients and customers through surveys, email campaigns, or feedback forms on your website. Use this feedback to identify areas for improvement and address any issues that may impact your reputation and the quality of your care.

At Zannis Plastic Surgery, we regularly solicit feedback from patients through satisfaction surveys and requests for feedback and online reviews after every appointment. This feedback loop allows us to identify areas for improvement and refine our brand experience to better meet client expectations. It also keeps us working hard to satisfy our patients and guests because there is no screening of potentially poor reviews. *Every* single patient after *every* visit is given the opportunity to review us, therefore *every* encounter must be as good as humanly possible!

Developing an Effective Marketing Strategy for Client Acquisition

Marketing today goes beyond traditional methods—it's about understanding your audience and leveraging various channels to connect with them effectively. Let's explore actionable steps to develop a successful marketing strategy.

1. Identifying Your Target Demographics:

Conduct thorough market research to identify your target demographics, preferences, and motivations. Understanding what drives clients to choose one aesthetic practice over another is essential for tailoring your marketing efforts effectively.

Your key target demographic could be female baby boomers (I know one of mine sure is). This group of potential customers shares certain desires and behaviors that must be well-understood if they are to be adequately reached and moved by your marketing efforts.[8]

2. Establishing a Strong Online Presence:

In today's digital age, having a strong online presence is crucial for attracting and retaining clients. This includes having a professionally designed user-friendly website that reflects your brand identity and showcases your services, facilities, and expertise,

Utilize and stay active on social media platforms such as Facebook, Instagram, and Twitter to connect with your audience, share updates about your med spa, and engage with followers. Post regularly, use visually appealing content, and encourage user-generated content and reviews to enhance credibility.

---

[8] Barletta, Marti. *Marketing to PrimeTime Women: How to Attract, Engage, and Convert the Boomer Big Spenders*. Kaplan Publishing, 2005.

Create informative and engaging content that educates and informs your target audience about medical spa treatments, skincare tips, and wellness advice. Publish blog posts, articles, videos, and infographics on your website and social media channels to showcase your expertise and attract potential clients.

Finally, don't forget to claim and optimize your business listings on local directories, review websites, and mapping services such as Google My Business, Yelp, and Bing Places. Ensure that your business information, including name, address, phone number, and hours of operation, is accurate and consistent across all platforms.

Dr. Sophia's Aesthetic Center maintains an informative website with detailed descriptions of their services, before-and-after galleries, and client testimonials. They also regularly post educational content on their social media platforms to engage with their audience and position themselves as industry experts.

3. Utilizing Traditional Methods:

While digital marketing is essential, traditional methods still have their place in a comprehensive marketing strategy. Partnering with local businesses, participating in community events, and distributing printed materials can help generate awareness and attract clients.

My first main marketing channel was billboard advertising, and today it's second only to Google ads. Billboard referrals are hard to track, but the presence they build in viewer's subconscious is undeniable. After meeting me for the first time, many people say, "Oh. . . I've seen your billboards."

4. Implementing Referral Programs:

Word-of-mouth marketing remains one of the most powerful tools for acquiring new clients. Implementing a referral program can incentivize existing clients to recommend your services to their friends and family.

Renew Beauty Studio offers a referral program where existing clients receive a discount on their next treatment for every new client they refer. This not only encourages client loyalty but also generates a steady stream of new leads through word-of-mouth referrals.

What's even more natural and powerful than such a referral program, is to provide your customers with a distinct reason why they have to share their experience with your practice. Make it so exceptional or unique, that patients are dying to spread the word organically.

5. Tracking and Analysis:

Regularly monitor and analyze the results of your marketing efforts using tools like Google Analytics. This data provides valuable insights into website traffic, conversion rates, and customer behavior, allowing you to refine your strategy based on real-time insights.

Glow MedSpa tracks the performance of their digital marketing campaigns using analytics tools. By analyzing metrics like website traffic, engagement rates, and conversion rates, they can identify which strategies are most effective and allocate their marketing budget accordingly.

Create Offers That Are Too Good to Refuse

Alex Hormozi, a renowned entrepreneur and investor, first captured my attention with his book *$100M Offers: How to Make Offers So Good*

People Feel Stupid Saying No[9]. It's a simple guide in which Hormozi distills his extensive experience and insights into creating irresistible offers that drive massive business growth.

The Foundation of a $100M Offer

At the heart of Hormozi's philosophy is the belief that a compelling offer is the cornerstone of business success. According to Hormozi, an offer is not merely a product or service but a **comprehensive value proposition that addresses the needs and desires of the target market**. To create a $100M offer, entrepreneurs must focus on four essential elements: the dream outcome, perceived likelihood of achievement, time delay, and effort and sacrifice.

1. **Dream Outcome**: This refers to the ultimate result that the customer desires. Hormozi emphasizes that understanding and articulating this dream outcome is crucial. Entrepreneurs need to tap into the emotional and aspirational aspects of their customers' desires, promising a transformation or significant improvement in their lives or businesses.

2. **Perceived Likelihood of Achievement**: Customers need to believe that the offer will deliver the promised results. Hormozi suggests building credibility through social proof, testimonials, and guarantees. By reducing the perceived risk, businesses can enhance the attractiveness of their offers.

3. **Time Delay**: The time it takes for customers to achieve the desired outcome is a critical factor. Hormozi advises minimizing this delay as much as possible, offering quick wins and fast results. The faster the customer can see progress, the more appealing the offer becomes.

---

[9] Hormozi, Alex. *$100M Offers: How to Make Offers So Good People Feel Stupid Saying No*. Acquisition.com, 2021.

4. **Effort and Sacrifice**: The less effort and sacrifice required from the customer, the more valuable the offer. Hormozi recommends making the process as effortless as possible, providing comprehensive support, resources, and guidance to ensure customer success with minimal friction.

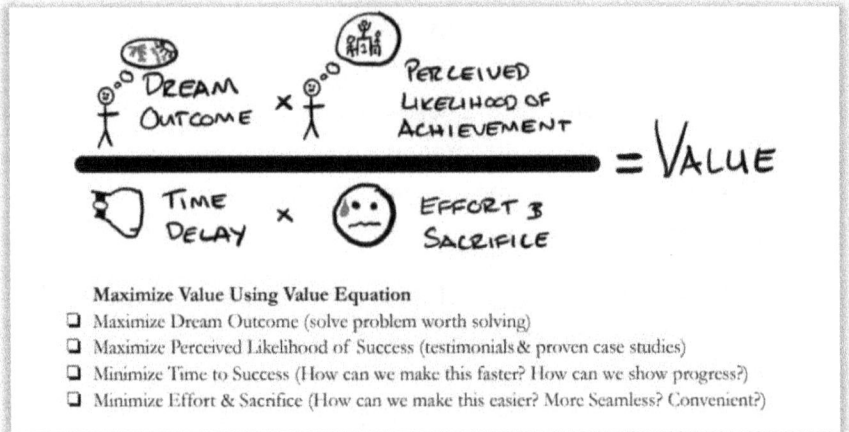

Figure 6. Hormozi's Value Equation. Image source: $100m Offers

Crafting the Irresistible Offer

Hormozi provides a step-by-step framework for crafting offers that customers find impossible to refuse. This involves several key strategies:

1. **Stacking Value**: He advocates for over-delivering on value by including additional features, bonuses, and benefits that exceed customer expectations. This approach creates a perception of immense value, making the offer too good to pass up.

2. **Pricing Strategy**: Pricing plays a pivotal role in how an offer is perceived. Hormozi encourages entrepreneurs to price their offers based on the value they provide rather than the cost. He also suggests using pricing psychology, such as anchoring higher prices against lower ones, to make the offer appear more attractive.

3. **Risk Reversal**: To further reduce the perceived risk, you should offer strong guarantees and risk-reversal mechanisms. Offering a money-back guarantee or a results-based guarantee reassures customers and builds trust.

4. **Creating Urgency**: Scarcity and urgency are powerful motivators. Consider using limited-time offers, exclusive deals, and bonuses for early adopters to create a sense of urgency that compels customers to act quickly.

Implementation and Scaling

Once an irresistible offer is crafted, the next step is implementation and scaling. As you will see in the next chapter highlighting Sabri Suby's philosophy, the importance of testing and iterating the offer based on customer feedback and market response can't be overstated. Continuous improvement and adaptation are crucial for maintaining the offer's effectiveness and staying ahead of competitors.

Additionally, Hormozi highlights the significance of a robust sales and marketing strategy to promote the offer. Leveraging multiple channels, such as social media, email marketing, and partnerships, can amplify reach and drive sales. Building a scalable infrastructure to support increased demand is also essential for sustained growth.

By focusing on creating immense value, reducing risk, and leveraging psychological triggers, you can craft offers that are virtually irresistible. Implementing these strategies not only drives sales but also fosters customer loyalty and long-term success.

Audience Engagement: Building a Loyal Client Base

Cultivating a loyal client base starts with understanding and engaging with your audience effectively.

1.Recognizing Client Needs:

Take the time to understand your clients' needs, preferences, and aspirations. Tailor your services and messaging to exceed their expectations and provide personalized experiences that resonate with them.

Bella Beauty Bar conducts client surveys and focus groups to gather feedback on their services and identify areas for improvement. By actively listening to their clients' needs and preferences, they can continuously refine their offerings and enhance the client experience.

2.Utilizing Effective Communication Channels:

Identify the communication channels preferred by your target audience and tailor your marketing efforts accordingly. Whether it's email newsletters, social media, or in-person events, choose channels that allow you to connect with your audience authentically.

Revive Wellness Center maintains an active presence on social media platforms like Instagram and Facebook, where they share behind-the-scenes glimpses, client testimonials, and educational content. This allows them to engage with their audience in a casual and relatable manner while showcasing their expertise and services.

3.Building Strong Relationships:

Building strong relationships with your clients is essential for fostering loyalty and repeat business. Take the time to connect with your clients on a personal level, show appreciation for their patronage, and provide exceptional customer service at every touchpoint.

Luxe Beauty Lounge goes above and beyond to make every client feel valued and appreciated. From personalized birthday gifts to handwritten thank-you notes, they consistently go the extra mile to show their clients how much they are appreciated.

4. **Seeking Feedback:**

Actively solicit feedback from your clients through surveys, reviews, and in-person conversations. This not only demonstrates that you value their opinions but also provides valuable insights into areas for improvement.

Radiant Skin Spa regularly sends out post-treatment surveys to gather feedback from their clients. They use this feedback to identify areas where they can enhance the client experience and ensure that every visit exceeds expectations.

Section 4: Leveraging Free Content on Social Media for Growth

Social media is a powerful tool for attracting new clients and expanding your business.

1. **Consistently Providing Value:**

Share valuable information, tips, and insights that showcase your expertise and provide value to your audience. Whether it's skincare tips, beauty tutorials, or behind-the-scenes glimpses, aim to educate and inspire your followers.

Bella Glow Skincare regularly posts educational content on their social media platforms, covering topics like skincare routines, ingredient spotlights, and common skincare concerns. By providing valuable information, they position themselves as trusted authorities in the skincare industry and attract followers who are interested in their services.

2. Tailoring Content for Platforms:

Each social media platform has its own unique features and audience demographics. Tailor your content to suit the platform and engage with your audience in a way that feels authentic and relevant.

Dr. Sarah's Dermatology Clinic shares before-and-after photos, client testimonials, and treatment videos on Instagram, where visual content performs best. On LinkedIn, they share industry insights, research studies, and professional achievements to engage with a more professional audience.

3. Engagement and Collaboration:

Foster a sense of community by engaging with your audience through likes, comments, and direct messages. Encourage user-generated content by reposting client photos and testimonials and inviting your followers to share their experiences.

Radiant Skin Spa hosts monthly Instagram challenges where followers can participate by sharing photos of their skincare routines or favorite products. This not only increases engagement but also creates a sense of camaraderie among their followers.

4. Collaboration and Partnerships:

Collaborate with influencers, local businesses, and industry experts to expand your reach and tap into new audiences. Whether it's hosting joint events, cross-promoting each other's content, or offering exclusive discounts, partnerships can help you reach new clients and strengthen your brand presence.

Glow Wellness Clinic partners with local yoga studios, fitness centers, and wellness influencers to host wellness workshops and events. These collaborations not only attract new clients but also position Glow Wellness Clinic as a trusted authority in holistic health and wellness.

By leveraging your free content on social media effectively, you can build a massive following and establish yourself as an authority in your field. Consistency, quality, engagement, and collaboration are the keys to success in social media marketing.

Chapter 10

Marketing from Down Under

"In the world of marketing, a compelling offer is your golden ticket."

— Sabri Suby

I work with a marketing genius and shark from Shark Tank Australia named Sabri Suby (founder of King Kong). His expertise and influence on me have been so profound that I decided to devote a chapter just on his proven strategies for digital marketing.

Sabri Suby Marketing to Sell Like Crazy:

1. **Focus on High-Impact Strategies:** In his book[10], Suby emphasizes the importance of identifying and focusing on high-impact marketing strategies that deliver measurable results. Rather than spreading resources thin across various channels, he advocates for concentrating efforts on tactics with the greatest potential for ROI.

2. **Understand Your Audience:** Suby stresses the significance of understanding your target audience deeply. By conducting thorough market research and customer analysis, you can gain insights into their needs, preferences, and pain points. This allows for more effective targeting and messaging in your marketing campaigns.

3. **Implement a Data-Driven Approach:** Suby advocates for using data and analytics to inform marketing decisions. By tracking key metrics and analyzing performance data, you can identify what's working well and

---

[10] Suby, Sabri. *Sell Like Crazy*. Sabri Suby, 2019.

where improvements can be made. This data-driven approach enables you to optimize your campaigns for better results.

4. **Embrace Automation and Scalability:** Suby emphasizes the importance of leveraging automation tools and systems to streamline marketing processes and scale your business efficiently. Automation can help save time, reduce manual workloads, and ensure consistency in your marketing efforts.

5. **Provide Value and Build Trust:** Suby emphasizes the importance of providing value to your audience through your marketing content. By offering valuable insights, education, and solutions to their problems, you can build trust and credibility with your audience, leading to stronger relationships and increased conversions.

6. **Test and Iterate:** Suby encourages marketers to adopt a mindset of continuous testing and iteration. Experiment with different strategies, messages, and tactics to see what resonates best with your audience. Use A/B testing and other methods to refine your approach and optimize performance over time.

7. **Invest in Education and Personal Growth:** Suby is a proponent of investing in education and personal development to stay ahead in the ever-changing landscape of digital marketing. By staying updated on industry trends, attending conferences, and seeking out mentorship, you can continuously improve your skills and knowledge.

Overall, Sabri Suby's teachings emphasize the importance of focusing on high-impact strategies, understanding your audience, leveraging data-driven insights, embracing automation, providing value, **testing and iterating**, and investing in education and personal growth to succeed in digital marketing.

Building a large social media following quickly:

Though not directly from Suby, I thought an exercise in building your legion of followers using his style of marketing would be helpful.

Building a large following on social media requires a combination of strategic planning, engaging content, and consistent effort. While there's no guaranteed way to gain a massive following overnight, here are some tips to help you grow your social media presence quickly:

1. **Define Your Niche and Audience:** Identify your target audience and niche market. Understand their interests, preferences, and pain points to create content that resonates with them. Tailor your messaging and branding to appeal directly to your target demographic.

2. **Optimize Your Profiles:** Ensure that your social media profiles are fully optimized with compelling bio, profile picture, and cover photo. Use relevant keywords and hashtags to make your profiles more discoverable in searches. Include links to your website or other relevant resources.

3. **Create High-Quality Content:** Focus on creating visually appealing, informative, and engaging content that adds value to your audience. Experiment with different formats such as videos, images, infographics, polls, and stories to keep your content fresh and diverse. Consistency is key—post regularly and at optimal times for maximum visibility.

4. **Leverage Influencers and Collaborations:** Partner with influencers, industry experts, or other brands in your niche to expand your reach and tap into their existing audience. Collaborations can help you gain exposure to new followers and build credibility through association with established figures or brands.

5. **Engage with Your Audience:** Actively engage with your followers by responding to comments, messages, and mentions promptly. Foster

conversations, ask questions, and encourage user-generated content to boost engagement and build a sense of community around your brand.

6.**Use Hashtags Strategically:** Research and use relevant hashtags to increase the discoverability of your posts and reach a broader audience. Experiment with popular and niche-specific hashtags to find the right balance between visibility and competition.

7.**Run Contests and Giveaways:** Host contests, giveaways, or challenges to incentivize engagement and attract new followers. Encourage participants to like, share, or tag friends to increase the reach of your content and drive organic growth.

8.**Invest in Paid Advertising:** Consider allocating a budget for social media advertising to reach a larger audience quickly. Platforms like Facebook, Instagram, and Twitter offer targeted advertising options that allow you to reach specific demographics based on interests, location, and behavior.

9.**Collaborate with Viral Content:** Keep an eye on trending topics, memes, and viral content within your niche. Create your spin on popular trends or participate in viral challenges to capitalize on the momentum and attract attention to your profile.

10. **Analyze and Iterate:** Monitor your social media analytics regularly to track your performance and identify what types of content resonate best with your audience. Use insights to refine your strategy, optimize your approach, and continue growing your following over time.

Remember, building a large social media following takes time, effort, and patience. It will not happen overnight. Focus on providing value, fostering meaningful connections, and staying authentic to your brand to attract and retain followers organically.

Chapter 11

Strategic Partnerships

"If you want to go fast, go alone. If you want to go far, go together."

— African Proverb

Collaboration with other businesses is a strategic approach to expand reach and enhance reputation. By partnering with skincare product manufacturers, wellness centers, influencers, and other relevant organizations, smaller businesses can eliminate competition, increase market share, and provide more comprehensive services to their customers. This chapter explores the benefits of such collaborations, how to identify and establish mutually beneficial partnerships, and the role of online collaborations with influencers.

The Importance of Collaborating with Other Businesses

If you're anything like me, you like to do everything yourself. You value other people's contributions, but you enjoy total creative control over the business you have built from the ground up. And, you don't really like sharing with other businesses.

However, collaboration between businesses offers several advantages that can drive growth and improve market positioning. Here are some key reasons why collaboration is important:

1. **Access to New Markets and Customers**: Partnering with businesses that cater to similar or complementary markets allows both parties to access a broader customer base. For example, a skincare product manufacturer collaborating with a wellness center can reach clients interested in holistic health and beauty treatments.

2. **Enhanced Credibility and Reputation**: Associations with reputable partners can enhance a business's credibility. When customers see that a business is working with well-known and respected companies, they are more likely to trust and choose that business.

3. **Resource Sharing and Cost Savings**: Collaborations can lead to shared resources, such as marketing budgets, expertise, and technologies. This can result in cost savings and improved efficiency for both parties.

4. **Innovation and Improvement**: Different businesses bring unique strengths and perspectives. Collaborative efforts can lead to innovation, improved products and services, and a more comprehensive value proposition for customers.

5. **Competitive Advantage**: By forming strategic alliances, businesses can reduce direct competition. This cooperative approach can lead to a more dominant market position and increased market share.

Identifying Potential Partners

Identifying the right partners is crucial for successful collaborations. Here are steps to identify potential partners:

1. **Analyze Your Business Needs**: Determine what your business lacks or what could be enhanced through collaboration. This could be new customer segments, technological capabilities, or additional expertise.

2. **Research Complementary Businesses**: Look for businesses that offer complementary products or services. For example, if you are a skincare brand, potential partners could include wellness centers, beauty salons, or fitness studios.

3. **Assess Compatibility**: Ensure that the potential partner shares similar values, goals, and target demographics. Compatibility is essential for a smooth and productive partnership.

4. **Evaluate Reputation and Reliability**: Research the potential partner's market reputation, financial stability, and track record. A reliable and well-regarded partner can significantly enhance your business's reputation.

5. **Seek Out Industry Events and Networks**: Attend industry conferences, trade shows, and networking events to meet potential partners. Joining professional associations and online industry forums can also help identify and connect with prospective collaborators.

Establishing Mutually Beneficial Partnerships

Once potential partners are identified, establishing a successful partnership involves several key steps:

1. **Initiate Contact and Build Relationships**: Reach out to potential partners with a well-thought-out proposal highlighting the benefits of collaboration. Building a relationship based on trust and mutual respect is fundamental.

2. **Define Clear Objectives and Goals**: Clearly outline the objectives of the partnership. Both parties should understand what they aim to achieve and how they will measure success.

3. **Negotiate Terms and Agreements**: Discuss and agree on the terms of the partnership, including roles, responsibilities, and resource allocation. It's essential to have a formal agreement or contract that outlines these details to avoid misunderstandings.

4. **Develop a Joint Marketing Strategy**: Create a collaborative marketing plan that leverages both businesses' strengths and resources. This could include co-branded campaigns, shared social media efforts, and joint events or promotions.

5. **Communicate Regularly**: Maintain open and regular communication throughout the partnership. This helps to address any issues promptly and ensures that both parties remain aligned with the partnership goals.

6. **Monitor and Evaluate**: Continuously monitor the performance of the partnership against the set objectives. Regular evaluations can help identify areas for improvement and ensure the collaboration remains beneficial for both parties.

Eliminating Competition Through Collaboration

Collaboration can be a strategic way to reduce competition. Here's how you can achieve this:

1. **Joint Ventures**: Forming a joint venture with a competitor can combine resources and expertise to create a stronger market presence. This approach can lead to increased market share and reduced competition.

2. **Strategic Alliances**: Developing strategic alliances with businesses that offer complementary products can create a more comprehensive service offering, making it harder for competitors to match.

3. **Exclusive Agreements**: Establishing exclusive agreements with partners can ensure that they do not collaborate with competitors. This can secure a unique market position and reduce competitive threats.

4. **Collaborative Innovation**: Working together on research and development can lead to innovative products and services that set both businesses apart from competitors.

Online Collaborations with Influencers and Organizations

In our digital age, online collaborations with influencers and organizations can significantly expand a business's reach. Here's how to effectively collaborate online:

1. **Identify Relevant Influencers**: Look for influencers whose followers align with your target demographic. The influencer should have a genuine connection to your industry and a reputation for authentic content.

2. **Establish Authentic Relationships**: Engage with influencers authentically. Building a genuine relationship ensures that the collaboration feels natural and resonates better with the audience.

3. **Define Collaboration Goals**: Clearly outline what you aim to achieve through the collaboration. This could be increased brand awareness, higher engagement, or boosted sales.

4. **Create Engaging Content**: Work with influencers to create content that is engaging and relevant to their followers. This could include product reviews, tutorials, giveaways, or sponsored posts.

5. **Utilize Multiple Platforms**: Collaborate with influencers across multiple platforms such as Instagram, YouTube, TikTok, and blogs. This multi-channel approach maximizes reach and impact.

6. **Leverage Influencer Networks**: Some influencers have networks of other influencers. Collaborating with one influencer can lead to introductions and collaborations with others, further expanding your reach.

7. **Measure and Analyze Results**: Track the performance of influencer collaborations using metrics such as engagement rates, website traffic, and sales conversions. Analyzing these results helps to understand the effectiveness of the partnership and guide future collaborations.

Case Studies and Examples

To illustrate the concepts discussed, here are some real-world examples of successful business collaborations:

1. **Sephora and Pantone**: Sephora, a leading beauty retailer, partnered with Pantone, the global authority on color, to create the "Color of the Year" cosmetics collection. This collaboration leveraged Pantone's expertise in color trends and Sephora's market reach to create a unique product line that attracted a broad customer base.

2. **GoPro and Red Bull**: The collaboration between GoPro, a manufacturer of action cameras, and Red Bull, an energy drink

company, is a prime example of a strategic alliance. Both brands share a target demographic interested in extreme sports and adventure. Their partnership includes co-branded events and content, such as the Red Bull Stratos project, which featured a skydiver breaking the sound barrier while wearing a GoPro camera.

3. **Nike and Apple**: Nike and Apple collaborated to create the Nike+ product line, which integrates Apple's technology with Nike's fitness products. This partnership combined Nike's expertise in sportswear with Apple's technological innovation, resulting in products that appeal to tech-savvy fitness enthusiasts.

4. **Starbucks and Spotify**: Starbucks partnered with Spotify to enhance the in-store experience for customers. Through this collaboration, Starbucks patrons could influence the music played in stores using the Starbucks app, and Spotify users could access exclusive Starbucks playlists. This partnership not only enhanced customer engagement but also integrated the digital and physical experiences.

Building Long-Term Collaborative Relationships

For collaborations to be successful in the long term, businesses need to focus on building and maintaining strong relationships. Here are some tips:

1. **Commitment to Mutual Success**: Ensure that the partnership is mutually beneficial and both parties are committed to each other's success. This involves understanding and supporting each other's goals.

2. **Transparency and Trust**: Maintain transparency in all dealings and foster a culture of trust. This means being honest about capabilities, limitations, and expectations.

3. **Flexibility and Adaptability**: Be prepared to adapt and evolve the partnership as needed. The business environment is dynamic, and being flexible can help the partnership thrive.

4. **Regular Check-ins and Reviews**: Schedule regular meetings to discuss progress, challenges, and opportunities. Continuous communication helps keep the partnership on track and address any issues early.

5. **Celebrate Successes Together**: Recognize and celebrate the successes of the collaboration. This helps build a positive relationship and motivates both parties to continue working together.

Conclusion

Collaborating with other businesses, such as skincare product manufacturers, wellness centers, and influencers, is a powerful strategy to expand reach and enhance reputation. By forming mutually beneficial partnerships, businesses can eliminate competition, increase market share, and provide more comprehensive services to their customers. The key to successful collaborations lies in identifying the right partners (as with all relationships!), establishing clear objectives, maintaining open communication, and continuously evaluating the partnership's effectiveness.

Online collaborations with influencers can further amplify these benefits, reaching a broader audience and driving growth. Through strategic collaborations, your business can achieve a competitive advantage and build a stronger, more reputable brand.

FINESSE

Scaling

Chapter 12

Financial Management & Profitability

"It's not how much money you make, but how much money you keep, how hard it works for you, and how many generations you keep it for."

— Robert Kiyosaki

Understanding Key Financial Metrics

To run a successful and profitable cosmetic surgery practice or spa, a deep understanding of key financial metrics is essential. These metrics provide valuable insights into the financial health and performance of your business, enabling you to make informed decisions and take strategic actions to drive growth and profitability.

If you're not a financial person, this can be an easy chapter to skip, but that would be a grave mistake. Many creative geniuses and incredible practitioners fail due to their poor understanding of financials. You should always have a snapshot of your business's financial health in your mind. Begin with learning the Key Performance Indicators (KPI's) for your business.

Gross Revenue Analysis:

Gross revenue represents the total income generated by your practice or spa. It is crucial to track revenue regularly and analyze trends over time to identify areas of growth or decline.

For example, Luxe MedSpa noticed a significant increase in revenue after introducing a new line of skincare products. By analyzing this trend, they identified the demand for high-quality skincare products among their clients and expanded their product offerings accordingly.

Cost of Goods Sold (COGS) Evaluation:

COGS encompasses all the direct costs incurred in providing your services, including surgical supplies, skincare products, and medical devices. Calculating the COGS allows you to determine the profitability of each service or product.

Dr. Smith's Cosmetic Surgery Clinic conducted a detailed analysis of their COGS and identified opportunities to negotiate better deals with suppliers, reducing their overall costs and increasing profitability.

Gross Margin Assessment:

Gross margin measures the profitability of your services or products after deducting the COGS. A high gross margin indicates a healthy profit margin, while a low gross margin may indicate the need for cost-cutting measures or pricing adjustments.

Radiant Beauty Spa achieved a high gross margin by offering premium skincare treatments at competitive prices. By focusing on high-margin services and optimizing their pricing strategy, they were able to increase their profitability significantly.

Operating Expenses Tracking:

Operating expenses include all the costs necessary to run your business, such as rent, utilities, salaries, marketing, and insurance. Tracking operating expenses allows you to identify areas of inefficiency and make necessary adjustments to reduce costs and improve profitability.

Glow Aesthetics Clinic implemented cost-saving measures such as energy-efficient lighting and digital marketing strategies to reduce their operating expenses. These initiatives helped them increase their bottom line while maintaining the quality of their services.

Profit and Loss (P&L) Statement Analysis:

P&L statements provide a comprehensive overview of your practice or spa's financial performance, including revenue, COGS, operating expenses, and net profit or loss. Regularly reviewing P&L statements allows you to identify trends, monitor financial health, and make informed decisions.

Renew Wellness Center used P&L statements to identify areas of inefficiency and reallocate resources to more profitable areas of their business. By optimizing their service offerings and streamlining operations, they were able to increase their profitability and achieve sustainable growth.

Implementing Effective Pricing Strategies

Effective pricing strategies are crucial for the success of cosmetic surgery practices and medical spas. Pricing your services appropriately ensures profitability and attracts and retains clients. Here are key factors to consider when implementing effective pricing strategies:

Know Your Costs:

Before setting prices, calculate the expenses involved in providing each service, including supplies, labor, and overhead. This will help you determine the minimum price necessary to cover costs and make a profit.

For example, Bella Skin Clinic analyzed the cost of their signature facial treatment, including labor, skincare products, and overhead expenses. Based on this analysis, they set a price that ensured profitability while remaining competitive in the market.

Research the Market:

Conduct a thorough market analysis to determine what your competitors are charging for similar services. This will give you insights into industry trends and help you position your prices competitively.

Dr. Johnson's Cosmetic Surgery Center regularly monitors competitor pricing and adjusts their pricing strategy accordingly. By offering competitive prices and value-added services, they attract clients and maintain a competitive edge in the market.

Consider Value Perception:

Pricing is not just about numbers; it is also about the perceived value of your services. Highlight the unique aspects of your services and communicate their value to justify premium pricing.

Luxe Beauty Spa positions itself as a luxury skincare destination by offering personalized treatments, high-quality products, and a serene spa environment. By emphasizing the luxury experience, they justify premium pricing and attract clients seeking a high-end skincare experience.

Tiered Pricing and Packages:

Implement tiered pricing or package options to cater to different client segments and maximize revenue. Create packages that offer varying levels of benefits and price points to appeal to a broader audience.

Glow MedSpa offers tiered membership packages that include a range of skincare treatments and discounts on products. By providing flexibility and value-added benefits, they attract clients looking for personalized skincare solutions while maximizing revenue.

Special Offers and Promotions:

Offering special promotions, discounts, or packages can be an effective way to attract new clients and incentivize repeat visits. Consider creating seasonal promotions, loyalty programs, or bundling services together to increase customer engagement and drive sales.

Radiant Beauty Clinic offers seasonal promotions such as holiday gift sets and discounted treatment packages. These promotions not only attract new clients but also encourage existing clients to book additional treatments, increasing revenue and client loyalty.

Test and Adjust:

Continuously monitor and analyze your pricing performance, making adjustments as needed. Experiment with different pricing models or promotional campaigns to identify what works best for your target audience.

Renew Wellness Spa regularly collects client feedback on pricing and service offerings through surveys and focus groups. Based on this feedback, they make adjustments to their pricing strategy to better meet client needs and preferences, ensuring continued growth and profitability.

Educate Your Staff:

Ensure that your staff understands the pricing strategy and can effectively communicate it to clients. Train them to address pricing inquiries or objections from clients and upsell value-added services when appropriate.

Bella Skin Clinic provides ongoing training to their staff on pricing strategy and effective sales techniques. By empowering their staff with knowledge and skills, they enhance the client experience and increase sales, contributing to overall profitability.

Maximizing Profitability through Cost Control and Revenue Optimization

Cost control and revenue optimization are integral aspects of running a business. By implementing effective cost control measures and optimizing revenue streams, you can increase profitability and achieve sustainable growth. Here are some techniques to reduce costs and optimize revenue:

Negotiate Better Deals with Suppliers:

Take the time to negotiate better deals with suppliers to reduce the cost of goods sold. Explore bulk purchasing options, negotiate volume discounts, and seek out alternative suppliers to lower costs without sacrificing quality.

Dr. Smith's Cosmetic Surgery Clinic renegotiated their contracts with suppliers and switched to more cost-effective alternatives for surgical supplies and skincare products. These efforts resulted in significant cost savings and increased profitability.

Optimize Inventory Management:

Implement inventory management systems to track inventory levels, minimize waste, and prevent stockouts. By optimizing inventory levels and reducing excess inventory, you can lower carrying costs and improve cash flow.

Luxe Beauty Spa implemented an inventory management system that tracks product usage and automatically generates purchase orders when inventory levels are low. This ensures that they always have the right products on hand, reducing waste and improving profitability.

Streamline Operational Processes:

Identify areas of inefficiency in your operational processes and streamline them to reduce costs and improve productivity. Automate routine tasks, eliminate unnecessary steps, and invest in technology solutions to streamline operations and save time and money.

Renew Wellness Center streamlined their appointment scheduling process by implementing an online booking system. This reduced administrative overhead, improved efficiency, and freed up staff to focus on client care, ultimately increasing profitability.

Optimize Service Offerings:

Analyze the profitability of your service offerings and focus on high-margin treatments or procedures. Consider discontinuing low-margin services or optimizing service bundles to maximize revenue and profitability.

Radiant Beauty Clinic conducted a profitability analysis of their service offerings and identified low-margin treatments that were not generating enough revenue to justify their costs. They replaced these treatments with higher-margin alternatives, increasing overall profitability.

Implement Marketing Strategies to Increase Revenue:

Invest in marketing strategies that drive revenue growth, such as targeted advertising campaigns, referral programs, and upselling techniques. Focus on attracting high-value clients and increasing the lifetime value of existing clients to maximize revenue.

Glow MedSpa launched a referral program that incentivizes existing clients to refer friends and family members by offering discounts on future treatments. This program not only attracts new clients but also encourages repeat visits, increasing overall revenue and profitability.

Focus on Customer Retention:

Invest in customer retention strategies to increase repeat business and lifetime customer value. Offer loyalty programs, personalized promotions, and exceptional customer service to keep clients coming back for more.

At Zannis Plastic Surgery, we use a loyalty app ("Zannis Rewards") created by a company that specializes in that service. It is a great platform that can be used to promote services, specials, sell packages, and every time a patients visits the office, they scan a QR code that tracks their progress towards multiple free gifts. Patients love it because it's modern, fun and really saves a lot of money, especially for frequent visitors. They can even share it with friends and both parties receive a free gift.

ZANNIS REWARDS

If you are a regular patient of ours or interested in self-care and beauty maintenance, our memberships are just for you. It's easy to join from our Zannis app and track your free rewards and monthly membership benefits. Choose from 4 popular plans and start saving hundreds to thousands of dollars on services you're already receiving!

TOX MEMBERSHIP	LASER MEMBERSHIP	GOLD MEMBERSHIP
$20/month	$99/month	$185/month
→ $9/unit Any Toxin	→ $9/unit Any Toxin	→ $9/unit Any Toxin
→ 10% OFF Skincare	→ 10% OFF Skincare	→ 10% OFF Skincare
→ 10% OFF Any Retail Item	→ 10% OFF Any Retail Item	→ 10% OFF Any Retail Item
	→ 20% OFF All Lasers	→ 20% OFF All Lasers & Body Contouring
Save over $400 / year		→ Choice of 1 Monthly: Hydrafacial, Chemical Peel, Laser Hair Removal
3 month commitment	Save up to $3,500 / year	
	6 month commitment	Unlimited Savings
		12 month commitment

Figure 7. Screenshot from www.zannisplasticsurgery.com/membership

By implementing these cost control measures and revenue optimization strategies, aesthetic practices can maximize profitability and achieve long-term success in the competitive aesthetics industry.

Continuously monitor financial performance, identify areas for improvement, and adapt strategies to changing market conditions to ensure sustained growth and profitability.

Chapter 13

Scaling Your Business

"As you grow, you learn more. If you stayed at a certain level, you wouldn't be able to experience all that you can, so I feel like you have to grow."

— Snoop Dogg

As a business owner in the aesthetic industry, scaling your practice is essential for growth and sustainability. Scaling allows you to reach more clients, increase revenue, and expand your impact. Here are some actionable strategies to help you scale your practice effectively:

Streamline Operations:

Start by assessing your current processes and workflows. Identify areas that can be improved or automated to increase efficiency and reduce costs. This could include implementing electronic medical records systems, streamlining appointment scheduling, or optimizing inventory management. By streamlining operations, you can free up time and resources to focus on growth initiatives.

Example: Dr. Smith's Medical Spa implemented a new EMR that streamlined patient intake processes, reducing administrative time by 30%. This allowed the staff to spend more time on patient care and marketing.

Develop a Strong Team:

Your team is the backbone of your practice. Invest in hiring and training competent staff members who align with your values and goals. Delegate responsibilities to capable individuals and empower them to take ownership of their tasks. A strong team can help you handle increased demand while maintaining exceptional patient care.

Example: Dr. Patel's Cosmetic Surgery Clinic implemented a rigorous training program for new staff members, focusing on patient communication, empathy, and clinical skills. As a result, the clinic's patient satisfaction scores improved, leading to higher client retention rates and increased referrals.

Enhance Marketing Efforts:

To attract more clients, you need to expand your reach and visibility. Develop a comprehensive marketing strategy that includes targeted advertising, social media campaigns, search engine optimization, and content marketing. Consider hiring a marketing specialist or outsourcing this aspect of your business to professionals who specialize in marketing for aesthetic practitioners.

Example: Dr. Nguyen's Aesthetic Center partnered with a digital marketing agency to launch a social media campaign targeting local residents interested in cosmetic procedures. The campaign generated a 20% increase in website traffic and a significant boost in client inquiries and bookings.

Expand Service Offerings:

Diversifying your service offerings is another opportunity for scaling your practice. Identify new treatments or procedures that align with your practice's expertise and clientele's demands. By expanding your services, you can attract a wider range of patients and increase revenue streams.

> **Example:** Dr. Rodriguez's Medical Spa introduced a new line of non-invasive body contouring treatments in response to growing demand from clients seeking alternative options to traditional liposuction. The new treatments proved to be highly popular, leading to a significant increase in revenue for the spa.

Foster Patient Loyalty:

Focus on providing exceptional patient experiences, personalized care, and effective communication. Implement loyalty programs, referral incentives, and post-treatment follow-ups to encourage repeat visits and word-of-mouth referrals.

Embrace Technology:

Leverage digital tools and software solutions to streamline various aspects of your practice, such as patient management, scheduling, billing, and record-keeping. By embracing technology, you can increase efficiency, reduce errors, and enhance the customer experience.

Example: Dr. Martinez's Dermatology Clinic implemented a telemedicine platform that allowed patients to schedule virtual consultations and follow-up appointments from the comfort of their homes. The platform improved access to care for patients and expanded the clinic's reach beyond its local area.

Exploring Opportunities for Expansion and Diversification

Expanding and diversifying your business will be essential for long-term growth. Here are some actionable steps to explore opportunities for expansion and diversification:

Stay Connected with Past Clients:

Your existing client base is a valuable source of business. Stay connected with past clients through email newsletters, social media engagement, and personalized follow-up messages. Offer special promotions or incentives to encourage them to return for additional treatments or refer their friends and family members.

Network and Collaborate:

Attend industry conferences, workshops, and networking events to connect with other professionals in the aesthetic industry. Build relationships with potential partners, collaborators, or investors who can help you expand your business. Consider joining professional organizations or associations to stay connected with industry trends and opportunities.

Develop and Sell Your Own Product Lines:

Creating your own line of skincare products or post-operative care supplies can be a lucrative opportunity for expansion. Identify gaps in the market and develop high-quality products that address the specific needs and preferences of your clientele. Leverage your existing client base to test and provide feedback on new products, and utilize your marketing channels to promote and sell your products online.

Example: I developed a line of medical-grade skincare products formulated with clinically proven ingredients. The flagship product (Glotopix™ rollerball serum) is marketed as complementary to our clinic's treatments, but primarily sold online through the Glotopix™ website and social media channels. The product has generated a significant source of additional revenue for the business and has helped gain customers from across the country.

Explore Additional Revenue Streams:

Consider diversifying your revenue streams by offering complementary services or partnering with other businesses in related industries. This could include offering spa services, aesthetician services, or wellness programs alongside your core medical services. Explore opportunities for affiliate marketing or sponsorship arrangements with companies that offer complementary products or services.

If You're the Only One, They Will Come

In the competitive world of cosmetic surgery and medical spas, differentiation is key to attracting and retaining clients. By establishing yourself as the go-to expert in a specialized niche, you can stand out from the competition and position yourself for success. Here's how to become the "only one" in your market:

Identify Your Niche:

Start by identifying a niche that aligns with your passion, expertise, and the needs of your target audience. This could be a specific surgical procedure, a particular target demographic, or a unique combination of services that sets you apart from other providers in your area.

Build Your Authority:

Once you've identified your niche, focus on building your authority and expertise in that area. Share your knowledge and insights through educational content, blog posts, social media posts, and speaking engagements. Position yourself as the go-to expert in your niche, and demonstrate your unique value proposition to potential clients. Maybe consider writing a book!

Deliver Exceptional Results:

To become the "only one" in your market, you need to deliver exceptional results that speak for themselves. Focus on providing top-notch patient care, personalized treatment plans, and outstanding outcomes that exceed your clients' expectations. By consistently delivering exceptional results, you'll establish yourself as the go-to provider in your niche.

Create a Unique Brand:

Differentiate yourself from the competition by creating a unique brand identity that reflects your niche and expertise. Develop a compelling brand story, logo, and visual identity that resonates with your target audience and sets you apart from other providers in your market. Your brand should convey trust, expertise, and a commitment to excellence.

Market Your Uniqueness:

Once you've established yourself as the "only one" in your niche, leverage your uniqueness to attract clients and grow your business. Showcase your expertise through targeted marketing campaigns, testimonials, before-and-after photos, and case studies that highlight your unique value proposition. By effectively communicating your uniqueness to potential clients, you'll attract more clients who are seeking the specialized services that only you can provide.

By becoming the "only one" in your market, you'll differentiate yourself from the competition, attract more clients, and position yourself for long-term success in the competitive world of cosmetic surgery and medical spas. Embrace your uniqueness, establish your authority, and **watch as clients flock to your practice because you're the only one who can provide the solutions they seek.**

FINESSE

Evolving

Chapter 14

Legal & Ethical Considerations

"In law, a man is guilty when he violates the rights of others. In ethics, he is guilty if he only thinks of doing so."

— Immanuel Kant

Understanding the legal and ethical landscape in the aesthetic industry is paramount for practitioners to ensure compliance, protect patients, and maintain the integrity of their practices. Let's delve deeper into the legal and ethical considerations, providing actionable advice and examples along the way.

Licensing and Scope of Practice:

Understanding licensing requirements and scope of practice regulations is fundamental for physicians, nurses, mid-level providers and medical spa owners. Each jurisdiction may have specific requirements, so practitioners must thoroughly research and comply with state and local laws. Most states require a medical director be responsible and readily available for any med-spa treatments (like cosmetic injectables or lasers).

Actionable Advice:

• **Research Licensing Requirements:** Take the time to understand the licensing requirements for cosmetic surgery and medical spa procedures in your area. This may involve contacting relevant regulatory bodies or consulting legal experts familiar with healthcare regulations.

• **Maintain Updated Licenses:** Ensure that all practitioners within your practice hold valid licenses and certifications. Keep track of expiration dates and renewal requirements to prevent any lapses in licensure.

• **Stay Informed About Scope of Practice:** Familiarize yourself with the scope of practice regulations governing your profession. Know which procedures you are legally permitted to perform and ensure that your practice operates within these boundaries.

• **Provide Ongoing Education:** Offer regular training sessions for staff members to ensure they understand licensing requirements and scope of practice regulations. This helps maintain compliance and promotes accountability within the practice.

Example: Dr. Garcia operates a cosmetic surgery clinic in California. Before opening his practice, he thoroughly researched the licensing requirements set forth by the California Medical Board and obtained the necessary licenses and permits. He also ensures that his staff members, including nurses and aestheticians, hold valid licenses and receive ongoing training to stay informed about changes in regulations.

Patient Privacy and Data Protection:

Protecting patient privacy and data is critical in the healthcare industry, including the field of cosmetic surgery and medical spas. Practices must adhere to strict privacy regulations, such as HIPAA, to safeguard patient information and maintain trust.

Actionable Advice:

• **Implement Secure Systems:** Invest in secure electronic medical record (EMR) software and other digital systems to store patient data securely. Ensure that these systems are regularly updated and undergo security assessments to prevent data breaches.

• **Train Staff on Privacy Protocols:** Provide comprehensive training to all staff members on HIPAA regulations and privacy best practices. Emphasize the importance of patient confidentiality and teach employees how to handle sensitive information responsibly.

• **Establish Data Access Controls:** Limit access to patient data to authorized personnel only. Implement role-based access controls and require strong passwords to prevent unauthorized access to patient records.

• **Conduct Regular Audits:** Regularly audit your data management systems to identify potential vulnerabilities and address any issues promptly. This helps ensure compliance with privacy regulations and reduces the risk of data breaches.

Real-Life Example:

Revive Wellness Spa employs stringent data protection measures to safeguard patient information. They use encrypted EMR software to store patient records securely and restrict access to authorized personnel only. Regular audits are conducted to assess the security of their systems and address any vulnerabilities.

3. Informed Consent:

Obtaining informed consent from patients is a legal and ethical requirement before performing any procedure or treatment.

Practitioners must ensure that patients fully understand the risks, benefits, and potential complications associated with the procedure.

Actionable Advice:

Develop Standardized Consent Forms: Create standardized informed consent forms for each procedure offered at your practice. These forms should clearly outline the procedure, associated risks, alternative treatments, and expected outcomes.

- **Educate Patients:** Take the time to educate patients about the procedure during the consultation process. Use layman's terms to explain complex medical concepts and encourage patients to ask questions to ensure they have a thorough understanding.

- **Encourage Questions:** Create a welcoming and supportive environment where patients feel comfortable asking questions and expressing concerns. Address any questions or doubts they may have and provide honest and transparent answers.

- **Document Consent Thoroughly:** Ensure that all informed consent discussions are documented in the patient's medical record. This documentation serves as evidence that the patient was adequately informed about the procedure and consented to treatment voluntarily.

Example: Dr. Lee, a plastic surgeon, conducts detailed consultations with each patient to discuss their treatment goals and explain the associated risks and benefits. He provides patients with informational materials and encourages them to take their time to review the information before making a decision. Dr. Lee documents the informed consent process in the patient's medical record to ensure compliance with legal and ethical standards.

Advertising and Marketing Compliance:

Advertising and marketing efforts in the cosmetic surgery and medical spa industry must comply with strict regulations to ensure transparency and protect consumers from misleading claims or promises. The American Society of Plastic Surgeons, for example, has strict guidelines for marketing and members must remain compliant.

Actionable Advice:

• **Understand Industry Regulations:** Familiarize yourself with advertising regulations specific to the cosmetic surgery and medical spa industry. Review guidelines provided by regulatory bodies or seek legal advice to ensure compliance.

• **Avoid Misleading Claims:** Refrain from making exaggerated claims or promises about the efficacy of treatments or procedures. Be honest and transparent in your marketing materials and avoid using language that may be misleading to consumers.

• **Use Before-and-After Photos Responsibly:** If using before-and-after photos in your marketing materials, ensure that they accurately represent the results achievable with your treatments. Obtain proper consent from patients and disclose any relevant information about the circumstances of the treatment.

• **Stay Up-to-Date:** Stay informed about changes in advertising regulations and adjust your marketing strategies accordingly. Regularly review and update your marketing materials to ensure compliance with the latest standards and guidelines.

Example: Elysian Aesthetics Clinic follows strict guidelines when advertising their services. They avoid making unrealistic promises or claims about their treatments and focus on providing accurate and informative content to educate consumers. Before-and-after photos used in their marketing materials are accompanied by disclaimers to ensure transparency and authenticity.

Staying Informed and Up to Date:

The legal and regulatory landscape in the cosmetic surgery and medical spa industry is constantly evolving. Practitioners must stay informed about changes in laws, regulations, and best practices to ensure compliance and provide the highest standard of care to their patients.

Actionable Advice:

• **Engage with Professional Organizations:** Join professional organizations or industry associations related to cosmetic surgery and medical spa practices. These organizations often provide resources, training, and updates on industry developments.

• **Attend Continuing Education Events:** Participate in continuing education seminars, workshops, and conferences to expand your knowledge and stay current on industry trends. Look for events that offer relevant information on legal and ethical considerations in aesthetic medicine.

• **Consult Legal Professionals:** When in doubt about legal or regulatory matters, seek advice from legal professionals or healthcare consultants who specialize in aesthetic medicine. They can provide guidance and clarification on complex issues and help ensure compliance with applicable laws and regulations.

> **Example:** Dr. Patel, a cosmetic surgeon, regularly attends conferences and seminars hosted by professional organizations such as the American Society of Plastic Surgeons (ASPS) to stay informed about changes in regulations and emerging trends in the field. He also consults with legal professionals to address any legal questions or concerns that arise in his practice.

So, always prioritize legal and ethical considerations to ensure compliance, protect patients, and maintain the integrity of their practices. Seek legal counsel whenever you have questions or concerns about your activities. By implementing actionable strategies and staying informed about changes in regulations, you can maintain professionalism and protect yourself against litigation too.

Chapter 15

Continuing Education and Growth

"Intellectual growth should commence at birth and cease only at death."

— Albert Einstein

Importance of Continuous Learning and Growth:

Continuous learning and professional development are foundational principles in the field of aesthetic medicine. In an industry where advancements occur rapidly, practitioners who prioritize ongoing education are better equipped to deliver high-quality care, stay abreast of emerging trends, and adapt to evolving patient needs.

Continuous learning goes beyond simply acquiring new skills or knowledge; it is a mindset that fosters innovation, excellence, and lifelong improvement. In aesthetic medicine, where patient safety and satisfaction are paramount, staying informed about the latest techniques, technologies, and best practices is essential for providing optimal outcomes and maintaining a competitive edge in the industry. In addition, all licensed medical practitioners are required to fulfill a minimum number of continuing education hours to maintain a valid license.

Actionable Advice:

• **Invest in Specialty Training:** Consider pursuing specialized training in areas such as injectables, laser treatments, or advanced surgical techniques. Specialty courses and workshops provide hands-on experience and in-depth knowledge that can enhance your expertise and differentiate your practice. Look for reputable training programs offered by accredited institutions or professional organizations.

• **Stay Informed about Regulations:** Regulatory compliance is a critical aspect of practicing aesthetic medicine. Stay abreast of changes and updates in regulations governing patient care, safety, and privacy. Attend regulatory compliance seminars or workshops to ensure that your practice remains compliant with laws and guidelines. Familiarize yourself with organizations such as the American Society for Aesthetic Plastic Surgery (ASAPS) and the American Academy of Dermatology (AAD) for guidance on regulatory standards and best practices.

• **Participate in Case Studies and Research:** Engage in clinical research or collaborate with researchers to contribute to the advancement of aesthetic medicine. Participating in case studies or research projects not only expands your knowledge but also adds credibility to your practice and establishes you as a thought leader in the field. Explore opportunities to publish case studies or present research findings at conferences and symposiums.

• **Mentorship and Preceptorship:** Seek mentorship from experienced practitioners or consider becoming a preceptor for aspiring aesthetic professionals. Mentorship provides valuable guidance, support, and opportunities for professional growth, while preceptorship allows you to share your expertise and contribute to the development of future practitioners. Look for mentorship programs offered by professional associations or academic institutions.

Real-Life Resources for Continuing Education:

• **American Academy of Cosmetic Surgery (AACS):** AACS offers a variety of educational resources and training opportunities for cosmetic surgeons, including live workshops, online courses, and certification programs. They also provide access to clinical practice guidelines, research publications, and networking events. Explore their website for a comprehensive list of educational offerings and membership benefits.

- **International Association for Physicians in Aesthetic Medicine (IAPAM):** IAPAM offers comprehensive training programs and workshops for physicians interested in aesthetic medicine. Their courses cover a wide range of topics, including injectables, laser treatments, and medical weight management. Check their calendar of events for upcoming training sessions and certification courses.

- **American Board of Cosmetic Surgery (ABCS):** ABCS offers board certification in cosmetic surgery, as well as continuing education resources and maintenance of certification programs. They provide access to educational materials, webinars, and conferences to support ongoing professional development. Visit their website for information on certification requirements and continuing education opportunities.

- **Local Medical Societies and Associations:** Explore opportunities for continuing education and networking through local medical societies and associations. Many regional organizations host educational events, meetings, and conferences specifically tailored to the needs of aesthetic practitioners in their area. Connect with your local chapter to stay informed about upcoming events and educational opportunities.

Networking and Collaborating with Industry Professionals:

Networking and collaboration are essential components of success in the field of aesthetic medicine. By building relationships with colleagues, industry experts, and related professionals, practitioners can gain valuable insights, share resources, and access new opportunities for growth and expansion.

Actionable Advice:

• **Build a Referral Network:** Cultivate relationships with other healthcare providers, such as dermatologists, primary care physicians, and OB-GYNs, who may refer patients to your practice for aesthetic treatments. Offer to collaborate on patient care and establish a referral network based on mutual trust and respect. Consider joining referral networks or professional alliances to expand your referral base.

• **Attend Multidisciplinary Meetings:** Participate in multidisciplinary meetings or conferences where professionals from different specialties come together to discuss complex cases or treatment options. These forums provide opportunities to collaborate, exchange ideas, and learn from experts in diverse fields. Look for conferences organized by organizations such as the American Society for Aesthetic Plastic Surgery (ASAPS) or the American Academy of Dermatology (AAD).

• **Join Networking Groups:** Join local or online networking groups specifically for aesthetic practitioners, where you can connect with colleagues, share experiences, and seek advice on clinical or practice management issues. Actively engage in discussions, attend meetups, and offer support to fellow members. Look for networking groups on platforms such as LinkedIn or Facebook, or consider starting your own group within your specialty or geographic area.

• **Collaborate on Educational Events:** Partner with other practitioners or organizations to host educational events, workshops, or seminars for patients or the community. Collaborative events not only provide valuable education but also showcase your expertise and strengthen your reputation as a trusted resource in the community. Consider partnering with local businesses, community centers, or schools to host events that educate the public about aesthetic medicine and promote your practice.

Chapter 16

Evolve and Adapt

"Change is the only constant in life. One's ability to adapt to those changes will determine your success in life."

— *Benjamin Franklin*

Change is inevitable. Predicting and preparing for change is ideal. But, most important is recognizing change and adapting to it in a manner that is healthy for your business and continues sustainable growth.

Eric Ries, in his excellent book *The Lean Startup*[11], provides a comprehensive framework for startups and established businesses alike to navigate uncertainty and achieve that coveted sustainable growth. By focusing on validated learning, experimentation, and iterative product development, he offers valuable insights into how businesses can evolve and adapt to changing market conditions and customer needs.

Let's explore the concepts of validated learning, the build-measure-learn feedback loop, minimum viable products (MVPs), pivoting, and innovation accounting. By understanding and implementing these strategies, businesses like yours can enhance their agility, minimize waste, and drive **continuous improvement**.

---

[11] Ries, Eric. *The Lean Startup: How Today's Entrepreneurs Use Continuous Innovation to Create Radically Successful Businesses*. Crown Business, 2011.

The Lean Startup Methodology

Validated Learning

At the heart of *The Lean Startup* is the concept of validated learning. Unlike traditional approaches that rely heavily on business plans and forecasts, validated learning emphasizes the importance of empirically testing assumptions about a product or business model. This process involves forming hypotheses, conducting experiments, and using the results to guide decision-making.

Validated learning helps businesses to:

- **Reduce Uncertainty:** By testing assumptions early, companies can avoid investing in ideas that are unlikely to succeed.

- **Focus on Customer Needs:** Understanding what customers truly want allows businesses to create products that address real problems.

- **Iterate Quickly:** Rapid experimentation enables businesses to learn and adapt faster than their competitors.

The Build-Measure-Learn Feedback Loop

The build-measure-learn feedback loop is a continuous cycle that drives the Lean Startup methodology. It involves three key steps:

1. **Build:** Develop a prototype or MVP that can be tested with real users.

2. **Measure:** Collect data on how users interact with the product and gather feedback.

3. **Learn:** Analyze the data to determine whether the initial assumptions were correct and decide on the next steps.

This iterative process ensures that businesses are constantly learning and improving. By focusing on small, incremental changes, companies can quickly adapt to new information and avoid costly mistakes.

Minimum Viable Product (MVP)

An MVP is a version of a new product that includes only the essential features needed to test the core assumptions. The goal is to quickly build a product that can be used to gather feedback and validate or invalidate hypotheses.

Benefits of using an MVP include:

- **Speed to Market:** Releasing an MVP quickly allows businesses to start learning from customers sooner.

- **Cost Efficiency:** By focusing on the most critical features, companies can minimize development costs.

- **Risk Reduction:** Testing with an MVP reduces the risk of building a product that no one wants.

Pivoting

Pivoting is the process of making a significant change to a product or business strategy based on the insights gained from validated learning. A pivot can involve altering the target market, changing the product's features, or even shifting the business model entirely.

Types of pivots include:

- **Zoom-in Pivot:** Focusing on a single feature of the product that has shown the most promise.

- **Zoom-out Pivot:** Expanding the product to include additional features that customers find valuable.

- **Customer Segment Pivot:** Targeting a different customer segment that may benefit more from the product.

Innovation Accounting

Innovation accounting is a method for measuring progress and ensuring accountability in the development process. It involves setting clear goals, defining metrics, and tracking progress over time. This approach helps businesses to:

- **Measure What Matters:** Focus on metrics that reflect real customer behavior and business outcomes.

- **Align Teams:** Ensure that everyone in the organization is working towards the same objectives.

- **Drive Continuous Improvement:** Use data to identify areas for improvement and guide future development efforts.

Applying Lean Startup Principles to Evolve and Adapt in Business

Embracing a Culture of Experimentation

To effectively evolve and adapt, businesses must foster a culture that encourages experimentation and learning. This involves:

- **Empowering Employees:** Allowing team members to take risks and test new ideas without fear of failure.

- **Encouraging Curiosity:** Promoting a mindset of continuous learning and curiosity about customer needs and market trends.

- **Celebrating Failures:** Viewing failures as opportunities to learn and improve, rather than as setbacks.

Leveraging Customer Feedback

Customer feedback is a crucial component of the Lean Startup methodology. Businesses can use customer insights to:

- **Refine Product Features:** Adjust product features based on what customers find most valuable.

- **Identify New Opportunities:** Discover unmet needs and potential new markets through customer interactions.

- **Improve Customer Satisfaction:** Continuously improve the customer experience by addressing feedback promptly.

Agile Development and Iteration

Agile development practices align closely with Lean Startup principles. By adopting agile methodologies, businesses can:

- **Respond Quickly to Change:** Agile practices enable teams to adapt to new information and market conditions swiftly.

- **Deliver Incremental Value:** Regularly releasing updates and new features ensures that customers receive ongoing value.

- **Enhance Collaboration:** Cross-functional teams can work more effectively together to solve problems and innovate.

Data-Driven Decision Making

Making decisions based on data rather than intuition is essential for adapting and evolving. Businesses should:

- **Establish Key Metrics:** Define the most important metrics that align with business goals and customer needs.

- **Analyze Performance:** Regularly review performance data to identify trends and areas for improvement.

- **Test Hypotheses:** Use A/B testing and other experimental methods to validate assumptions and guide decisions.

Scaling Successfully

As businesses grow, maintaining the agility and adaptability of a startup becomes more challenging. To scale successfully while remaining adaptable, companies should:

- **Maintain Lean Practices:** Continue to apply Lean Startup principles to new projects and initiatives.

- **Invest in Technology:** Leverage technology to automate processes and enhance data analysis capabilities.

- **Foster a Learning Culture:** Encourage ongoing learning and development for employees at all levels.

Case Studies and Real-World Examples

Several companies have successfully applied Lean Startup principles to evolve and adapt in their respective industries. Notable examples include:

Dropbox

Dropbox used an MVP to test their product concept before investing heavily in development. They created a simple video demonstrating the functionality of their file-sharing service, which generated significant interest and validated the demand for their product. This approach allowed Dropbox to refine their product based on real user feedback and grow rapidly.

Airbnb

Airbnb started with a basic MVP by renting out air mattresses in their apartment during a conference. This initial experiment helped them understand the market demand and customer preferences. By continuously iterating and responding to feedback, Airbnb was able to expand their platform and disrupt the traditional hospitality industry.

Zappos

Zappos tested the viability of their online shoe store by setting up a simple website and listing products without holding inventory. When a customer placed an order, they would purchase the shoes from a local store and ship them directly to the customer. This approach validated the demand for online shoe shopping and informed their future business strategy.

Conclusion

Fostering a culture of experimentation, leveraging customer feedback, adopting agile development practices, making data-driven decisions, and maintaining lean practices during scaling are the keys to applying Lean Startup principles. The examples we looked at from companies like Dropbox, Airbnb, and Zappos demonstrate the effectiveness of this approach in driving innovation and major growth.

I began this chapter with a famous quote from Benjamin Franklin. I'd like to conclude it with a lesser known one from one of my role models:

"All fixed set patterns are incapable of adaptability or pliability. The truth is outside of all fixed patterns." — *Bruce Lee*

Chapter 17

Building a Multimillion-Dollar Business

"Screw it, let's do it."

—Richard Branson

Congratulations on making it to the final section! It's clear that you're serious about taking your business to the next level. Throughout this book, we've delved into various strategies, tips, and techniques to help you build a multimillion-dollar business empire in the aesthetic industry. While this outline provides a roadmap, the true magic happens in the execution.

First and foremost, remember that every successful business empire is built on a solid foundation. This foundation begins with a clear vision and mission for your practice. Define your goals, pinpoint your target market, and develop a unique selling proposition that distinguishes you from your competitors.

But the nitty gritty details are what make it actually happen. Take each section we've covered and flesh it out into a step-by-step guide of exactly what you should do and how. No vague theories here—just precise action steps that you will implement.

The Billionaire Mindset

Billionaires often possess certain traits and adopt specific mindsets that set them apart from the average person. While individual characteristics may vary, here are some common attributes and behaviors that distinguish billionaires from the general population:

1. **Visionary Thinking:** Billionaires tend to have a long-term vision and the ability to think big. They envision possibilities beyond the status quo and set ambitious goals that drive them to achieve extraordinary results. Their vision guides their decisions and actions, propelling them forward even in the face of adversity.

2. **Risk-Taking:** Billionaires are willing to take calculated risks to pursue their goals and dreams. They understand that success often requires stepping outside of one's comfort zone and embracing uncertainty. Rather than being deterred by failure or setbacks, they view them as valuable learning experiences that contribute to their growth and resilience.

3. **Entrepreneurial Mindset:** Many billionaires have an entrepreneurial mindset characterized by creativity, innovation, and a bias towards action. They identify opportunities where others see challenges and are quick to capitalize on emerging trends and market gaps. They are not afraid to challenge the status quo and disrupt traditional industries with groundbreaking ideas and solutions.

4. **Resilience and Persistence:** Building wealth and achieving success often requires resilience and persistence in the face of obstacles and setbacks. Billionaires possess a relentless drive to overcome challenges and persevere in pursuit of their goals. They maintain a positive attitude, learn from failures, and adapt their strategies to navigate changing circumstances.

5. **Focus on Value Creation:** Billionaires prioritize value creation over short-term gains or personal enrichment. They focus on building businesses and enterprises that solve meaningful problems, improve people's lives, and create lasting impact. By delivering exceptional value

to customers, employees, and stakeholders, they lay the foundation for sustainable growth and success.

6. **Continuous Learning:** Billionaires have a thirst for knowledge and a commitment to lifelong learning. They recognize that staying informed and adapting to new developments is essential for remaining competitive in a rapidly evolving world. They invest in education, surround themselves with smart and knowledgeable people, and actively seek out opportunities for personal and professional growth.

7. **Strategic Thinking:** Billionaires are strategic thinkers who carefully analyze situations, anticipate future trends, and develop well-thought-out plans of action. They make decisions based on data, market insights, and calculated risk assessments rather than relying solely on intuition or emotion. Their strategic approach enables them to capitalize on opportunities and navigate complex business environments with confidence.

8. **Generosity and Philanthropy:** Many billionaires are known for their philanthropic efforts and commitment to giving back to society. They recognize their privilege and use their wealth and influence to make a positive impact on causes they care about. By supporting charitable initiatives, funding research, and advocating for social change, they contribute to building a better world for future generations.

Overall, billionaires possess a combination of vision, courage, resilience, and strategic thinking that sets them apart from the average person. While not everyone may aspire to reach billionaire status, adopting some of these mindset and behavior traits can help you unlock your full potential and achieve greater success in your personal and professional life.

Appendix: References, Resources and Tools

"The appendix may be useless, but it's not an organ without a cause. Its primary function is to teach us humility."

— Unknown

References:

1. Collins, Jim. *Good to Great: Why Some Companies Make the Leap... and Others Don't.* Harper Business, 2001.

2. Kim, W. C., & Mauborgne, R. (2005). Blue ocean strategy: How to create uncontested market space and make the competition irrelevant. Harvard Business School Press.

3. Ries, Al, and Jack Trout. Positioning: The Battle for Your Mind. McGraw-Hill, 2001.

4. Godin, Seth. Purple Cow: Transform Your Business by Being Remarkable. Portfolio, 2003.

5. Kondo, Marie. *The Life-Changing Magic of Tidying Up: The Japanese Art of Decluttering and Organizing.* Ten Speed Press, 2014.

6. Solomon, Micah. *The Heart of Hospitality: Great Hotel and Restaurant Leaders Share Their Secrets.* Select Books, Inc., 2016.

7. Barletta, Marti. *Marketing to PrimeTime Women: How to Attract, Engage, and Convert the Boomer Big Spenders.* Kaplan Publishing, 2005.

8. Hormozi, Alex. *$100M Offers: How to Make Offers So Good People Feel Stupid Saying No.* Acquisition.com, 2021.

9. Suby, Sabri. *Sell Like Crazy.* Sabri Suby, 2019.

10. Ries, Eric. *The Lean Startup: How Today's Entrepreneurs Use Continuous Innovation to Create Radically Successful Businesses*. Crown Business, 2011.

Other Recommended Books:

1. Russell, J. (2011). *Building a Medical Spa: An Insider's Guide to Success*. Medical Spa MD Publishing.

This book delivers insights from industry experts and covers topics such as financial planning, staffing, and legal considerations.

2. Covey, A. J. (2009). Med Spa Confidential: Starting and Running Your Own Cosmetic Practice. CreateSpace Independent Publishing Platform.

Offers practical advice from an experienced cosmetic physician on starting and managing a med spa.

3. Kihm, J. T. (2015). The Business of Medical Spa: How to Create a World-Class Medical Spa. Lulu Publishing Services.

This guide provides step-by-step instructions on creating a successful med spa, covering business planning, marketing, and operational strategies.

4. Sawyer, T. (2018). Med Spa Marketing Secrets: Online Marketing Techniques to Attract and Convert More Patients. CreateSpace Independent Publishing Platform.

Focused on marketing, this book provides strategies to enhance online presence and attract more clients to a med spa.

5. Linden, A., & Linden, R. (2018). Financially Intelligent Med Spa: How to Start, Manage, and Grow a Profitable Aesthetic Practice. Independently published.

This book focuses on the financial aspects of running a med spa, from startup costs to long-term profitability strategies.

Websites:

1. American Society of Plastic Surgeons (ASPS) – The ASPS website is a valuable resource for cosmetic surgeons, providing access to industry news, research articles, educational materials, and networking opportunities.

2. Medical Spa MD – This online community for medical spa owners and practitioners is an excellent platform to connect with peers, share experiences, and gain insights into the latest trends, technologies, and best practices in the industry.

3. RealSelf – A popular website that allows patients to research and review cosmetic treatments and practitioners. This platform provides valuable feedback on patient experiences and can help you understand patient expectations and preferences.

4. John Zannis, MD – Author's educational site for business growth, aesthetic practice support and med-spa development. Includes online courses and coaching opportunities. www.zannis.com

Digital Downloads:

1. 10 Best Marketing Strategies for Cosmetic Surgeons – You can choose to compete with the crowd, or distinguish yourself and your services with quality online content like blogs, videos, and social media posts that actually help prospective patients and ultimately lead them to you!
https://www.zannis.com/10-best-plastic-surgery-marketing-strategies

2. Spa Owner's Guide to Hiring Top Talent – Learn how to find the hidden gems that will be superstars for your business and keep happy customers coming to you for years.
https://www.zannis.com/spa-owner-s-guide-to-hiring-top-talent

www.ingramcontent.com/pod-product-compliance
Lightning Source LLC
Chambersburg PA
CBHW070041100426
42740CB00013B/2746